Altcoins For Beginners 2021

Copyright Notice:

No part of this publication may be reproduced, distributed, or transmitted in any form or by any means, including photocopying, recording, or other electronic or mechanical methods, without the prior written permission of the publisher, except in the case of brief quotations embodied in critical reviews and certain other noncommercial uses permitted by copyright law. For permission requests, contact the publisher:

Copyright © 2021 All rights reserved.

Disclaimer:

The information provided in this book is for informational purposes only and is not intended to be a source of advice or credit analysis with respect to the material presented. The information contained in this book do not constitute legal or financial advice and should never be used without first consulting with a financial professional to determine what may be best for your individual needs.

The publisher and the author do not make any guarantee or other promise as to any results that may be obtained from using the content of this book. You should never make any investment decision without first consulting with your own financial advisor and conducting your own research and due diligence. To the maximum extent permitted by law, the publisher and the author disclaim any and all liability in the event any information, commentary, analysis, opinions, advice and/or recommendations contained in this book prove to be inaccurate, incomplete or unreliable, or result in any investment or other losses.

Content contained or made available through this book is not intended to and does not constitute legal advice or investment advice and no attorney-client relationship is formed. The publisher and the author are providing this book and its contents on an "as is" basis.

DEDICATION

Dedicated to those who believe that competition is beneficial for the free markets.

CONTENTS

Part 1	Introduction To Altcoins	
Part 2	Bitcoin Review	
Part 3	The Altcoins	
Part 4	How to Invest in and Store Altcoins	
Part 5	Conclusion Who Wins The Battle of Altcoins vs. The Bitcoin King?	

Detailed Table of Contents

PART 1 – INTRODUCTION TO ALTCOINS

Chapter 1 - Investing in AltCoins - What You Should Know About Decentralized Currencies

Chapter 2 - A Primer On Different Cryptocurrencies For Beginners

Chapter 3 - An Overview of Efficient Altcoins

PART 2 – BITCOIN REVIEW

Chapter 4 - Behind The Bitcoin Price

Chapter 5 - How Is the Supply of Bitcoins Selected?

PART 3 – THE ALTCOINS

Chapter 6 - Meet The Contenders

Chapter 7 - The Vitality Of The Ethereum Smart Contract

Chapter 8 - Why Invest in in the Ethereum token, ERC20?

Chapter 9 - What Is Cardano?

Chapter 10 – Cardano's Advanced Proof Of Stake

Chapter 11 - What Are Stablecoins?

Chapter 12 - Which Are the Best Stablecoins?

Chapter 13 - Trading Stablecoins

Chapter 14 - Tether Currency and Commodity Indexes Can Be Investment Bridges For Crypto Investors

Chapter 15 - Binance Coin: Altcoin Associate With A Crypto Exchange

Chapter 16 - Binance Smartchain

Chapter 17 - Ripple Protocol For Financial Institutions and Investors

Chapter 18 - Validation of Transactions on the XRP Market

Chapter 19 - Dogecoin: A Boon to Cryptocurrency Investors

Chapter 20 - How Dogecoin Marketing Can Improve Its Popularity

Chapter 21- Why Buy Polkadot?

Chapter 22 - Solana Core Developers - Discusses How They Made a Difference With Their Proof of Stake Model

Chapter 23 – Solana: The New Cryptocompetition

Chapter 24 - What Is Uniswap and How Does It Work?

Chapter 25 – Uniswap: A Hybrid Investment Platform

Chapter 26 - Learning More About the Bitcoin Cash (BCH)

Chapter 27 – BCH: a stable and secure Bitcoin fork

Chapter 28 – Litecoin is Still One of the Fastest Growing Altcoins

Chapter 29 - Litecoin: The Original Crypto 'Silver'

Chapter 30 – Chainlink for Hybrid Smart Contracts

Chapter 31 - Using Chainlink For Your Cryptocurrency Project

PART 4 – HOW TO INVEST IN AND STORE ALTCOINS

Chapter 32 - What Popular Cryptocurrency Exchanges Have in Common

Chapter 33 - Compare the Best Cryptocurrency Exchanges For Your Trading Needs

Chapter 34 - Binance - A New Trading Way For the Cryptocurrency Market

Chapter 35 – Binance Can Exchange Dollars For Your Favorite Altcoins

Chapter 36 - Using Coinbase to Trade or Invest in Cryptocurrencies

Chapter 37 – Cryptocurrency Wallets - What Are The Benefits and Drawbacks?

Chapter 38 - A New Transparency in the Lives of Cryptocurrency Consumers

Chapter 39 - Advantages Of Nano Ledger Software Wallets

PART 5 – CONCLUSION: WHO WINS THE BATTLE OF ATLCOINS VS THE BITCOIN KING?

Chapter 40 – More About Altcoins – The Alternative Cryptocurrencies

Chapter 41 - A Brief Review of Cryptocurrencies

Chapter 42 - Using Dollar Cost Averaging Strategies For Your Crypto Portfolio

Chapter 43 - Using More Dollar Cost Averaging Strategies

Chapter 44 - Dollar Cost Averaging: A Great Option For Long Term Investing

Chapter 45 - Making Long Term Crypto Investments

Chapter 46 - Benefits of Investing in Cryptocurrencies

PART 1 – INTRODUCTION TO ALTCOINS

Altcoins, as the name suggests, are alternative cryptocurrencies that do not operate on the Bitcoin protocol. In this book, you will learn about many of the most popular and heavily traded altcoins. The primary altcoins discussed in this book are all in the top 15 in terms of market capitalization at the time of this publication. The current cryptocurrency leaders are updated regularly on www.coinmarketcap.com, so it is recommended to check that website for cryptocurrency pricing and market capitalization updates. As you'll soon discover in this book, many of these top 15 contenders have the potential to hold or improve their positions in the cryptocurrency standings in the years ahead. And some may even have the potential to displace the Bitcoin King for the #1 spot.

Chapter 1 - Investing in AltCoins - What You Should Know About Decentralized Currencies

Altcoins are a type of digital currency that exists outside of the bitcoin protocol. The word altcoin is short for alternate currency as in, another form of digital currency. There are several different altcoins, and they are all different from bitcoins. However, they are not physical coins. Instead, they exist as virtual assets on the Internet.

Most people who are new to the world of investing do not realize that several different currencies can be traded. Some are worth more than others depending upon your risk appetite. Altcoins are simply an alternate form of currency that has been traded on the Internet. Altcoins can be traded on online brokers and they have gained a lot of popularity in recent years.

You'll learn a lot about altcoins in this book, but before investing it's probably a good idea to visit the website for each one with a quick Google search. There you will find out more information, including information on the different types of whitepapers written by their founders.

For example, Litecoin is a form of digital currency that was created as an improvement on the Bitcoin protocol. This particular altcoin has not gone through a significant upgrade, but for many years since the emergence of cryptocurrencies, Litecoin was known as "Silver" while Bitcoin was considered analogous to "Gold".

For those readers who are new to investing in general, if you are going to invest in any altcoins, it is recommended to seek professional financial advice before doing so. This is because not every investment is right for everyone. Some people are simply not good candidates for this type of investing. It should be noted that this is not just about investing in altcoins but also in general. If you do not want to risk your money, then it is important to get the proper advice before making any decisions whatsoever. Most experts agree, that it is not recommended to invest more than 5 to 10 percent of your total assets in cryptocurrency. They continue to be highly speculative, so be careful.

For those readers that are ready to invest carefully and wisely, let's continue. In addition to a brief Bitcoin review, the primary altcoins that will be discussed in this book include Ethereum, Cardano, Binance coin, Stablecoins, Ripple, Dogecoin, Polkadot, Solana, Uniswap, Bitcoin Cash, Litecoin, and Chainlink.

It is recommended to read this book from beginning to end, and later you can also use it as a reference to reread more about your favorite cryptos with the table of contents menu

Chapter 2 - A Primer On Different Cryptocurrencies For Beginners

Cryptocurrency altcoins for beginners, what are they? Well, an altcoin is a new digital currency that is mined with the intention of creating more out of computer code. There are thousands of such coins because anyone who understands computer code can create their own. However, most of these will not be valuable and should be avoided. For this reason, the altcoin cryptocurrencies that are discussed in this book are the ones most favored by institutions. The altcoins discussed in the book are the cryptocurrencies that are most likely to perform best in the near future and possible long term future because these are among the top 15 cryptocurrencies on www.coinmarketcap.com, and so you know that their market capitalization is high and the interest in them from institutional investors is exceptional.

Before we delve into the details, you need to know about the cryptosystem itself. Many people believe that Cryptocurrencies are "Fiat currencies". This isn't true at all. Here, you will learn about the advantages and disadvantages of this type of Cryptocurrency exchange.

Some of the most popular altcoin cryptocurrencies exchanged today include ethereum, Cardano, Binance coin, chainlink, Uniswap, and Litecoin. We'll go into details on each of these as we progress through the chapters of this book. Many of these altcoins are created nowadays using special software that makes the process of mining easy and fast. So, if you want to earn profits, you need to do is download some such software from the Internet and then install them on your PC.

But beware, that mining cryptocurrencies is a complex topic and requires a substantial investment in hardware, including those required for safety precautions. Cryptocurrency mining is becoming more difficult as the years pass, and now there are often mining farms where this occurs in special facilities.

Crypto mining works best in cooler climates where electricity costs are lowest, so it may not be optimal for everyone.

It also requires a significant upfront investment in hardware.

For the average consumer, cryptocurrency mining nowadays may not be worth the effort. It is likely much easier to participate in the altcoin market by simply buying (or selling) these cryptocurrencies on exchanges, so that'll what we'll focus on in this book.

Buying Altcoins is usually done via Cryptocurrency Exchanges. There are several well-known and reputable Altcoin Exchanges like Binance.us and Coinbase for US investors, and Binance.com for investors outside the US.

When selecting an altcoin to buy, it's smart to choose one based on two factors: the amount of money you can afford to invest, and the reputation of the marketplace that you are considering. If you have a lot of money to spend, then you should go for a high-quality marketplace such as those offered by the top right currencies in the world. To get the highest possible price, you can visit various online trading platforms and compare prices. This will allow you to pick out the best price per currency based on your own needs and preferences.

Larger exchanges such as those based in the US or the UK are good places to go for a variety of reasons. These are because these types of exchanges do not typically allow for the trading of lesser coins.

Each of the reputable cryptocurrency exchanges has regulatory requirements that they must meet, so your ability to use a certain exchange for cryptocurrencies may depend on your geographical location.

Chapter 3 - An Overview of Efficient Altcoins

Generally speaking, altcoins function very similarly to the original Bitcoin. With a private key, you could send a transaction from your online digital wallet to another online user's private key. However, in a more Cryptocurrency like these, a blockchain, or block recording ledger, where all the transactions are publicly and forever recorded, exchanges cannot be changed or blocked after the fact. This is also how the original Internet Currency would work.

Altcoins are not supported by the official infrastructure of the creators of the coins. As a result, there is no central organization or group which governs it. In the case of the Internet currency, it is called the WebEx, and in altcoins, it is called the Maidoken. But there are other names for it, and the one that will be used here is the Feudal Internet Currency.

There are two major differences between altcoins and traditional Internet currency. The first difference is in the level of privacy or confidentiality of the transactions. Unlike in the traditional Internet currency, altcoins provide their users with low transaction fees. Since the main purpose of altcoins is to emulate the characteristics of the original, its users will have to deal with some disadvantages.

One of them is that they are not supported by any regulatory authority. This is why the total number of altcoins has remained relatively low, compared to the number of currencies that have been launched. As a result, their price is subject to fluctuations. Sometimes they increase, sometimes they decrease. Because of this, the number of fraudulent transactions has become quite high.

Another problem faced by users of altcoins is the possibility of their confiscation, especially in some countries like China. In the case of the original chain, the miners are the ones who control the supply of coins, while altcoins are "mined" or produced using a different method. Altcoins based on the original protocol will always have more value than those that are mined through a different method.

Furthermore, because of the way the algorithm is implemented, some users believe that it is impossible to create a truly decentralized form of currency. Although it is difficult to build decentralized AltCoins, it is not impossible to build tokens that have some characteristics of decentralized AltCoins. For instance, although there are currently no legal restrictions on creating AltCoins, the law might someday change that makes it necessary for users to follow certain rules. Also, although it would be very difficult to change the existing legal framework for creating AltCoins, it would be possible to create new legal solutions for the decentralized aspect of currencies. One example is exchanging money through an automated machine, which would allow people to exchange one currency for another without much hassle.

While these problems cannot be ignored, the developers of these new blockchains hope that in time their algorithms will overcome these obstacles and make it possible to offer a true decentralization of tokens on the market. One example of this solution is ethereum, the first self-governing digital network in the world. The reason why many experts consider ethereum a good choice for tokens is that it uses a hybrid form of distributed computing technology, called Proof-of-Work, along with its digital currency, called ether. The two technologies work hand-in-hand, with ether being used as a source of incentives for users while the Proof-of-Work is used as a source of computing power which validates the legitimacy of the network. Because the developers of Ethereum ran an extensive trial during the early stages of development, it is now among the most powerful networks in its field.

In addition to its smart contract features, ether is also meant to be used as a bridge cryptocurrency between other currencies. This is why ethereum is such a good option for altcoin beginners - to give them a chance to learn how their system works from the ground up. Another reason that ethereum makes a good choice for tokens is that it allows users to transact with relative ease. In the coming months, we are sure to see a lot of growth in this space thanks to the innovations of smart contract programming.

PART 2 – BITCOIN REVIEW

Bitcoin was introduced in great detail in Book 1 of this *Cryptocurrency Explained Simply* Book Series. If you need a refresher, it may be a good idea to take another look at Book 1: ***Bitcoins, Blockchains and Smart Contracts***. For completeness of this current Book 2, and before getting into the details on its primary competitors, let's just do a quick review here on this critical cryptocurrency and current title holder: the Bitcoin King.

Chapter 4 - Behind The Bitcoin Price

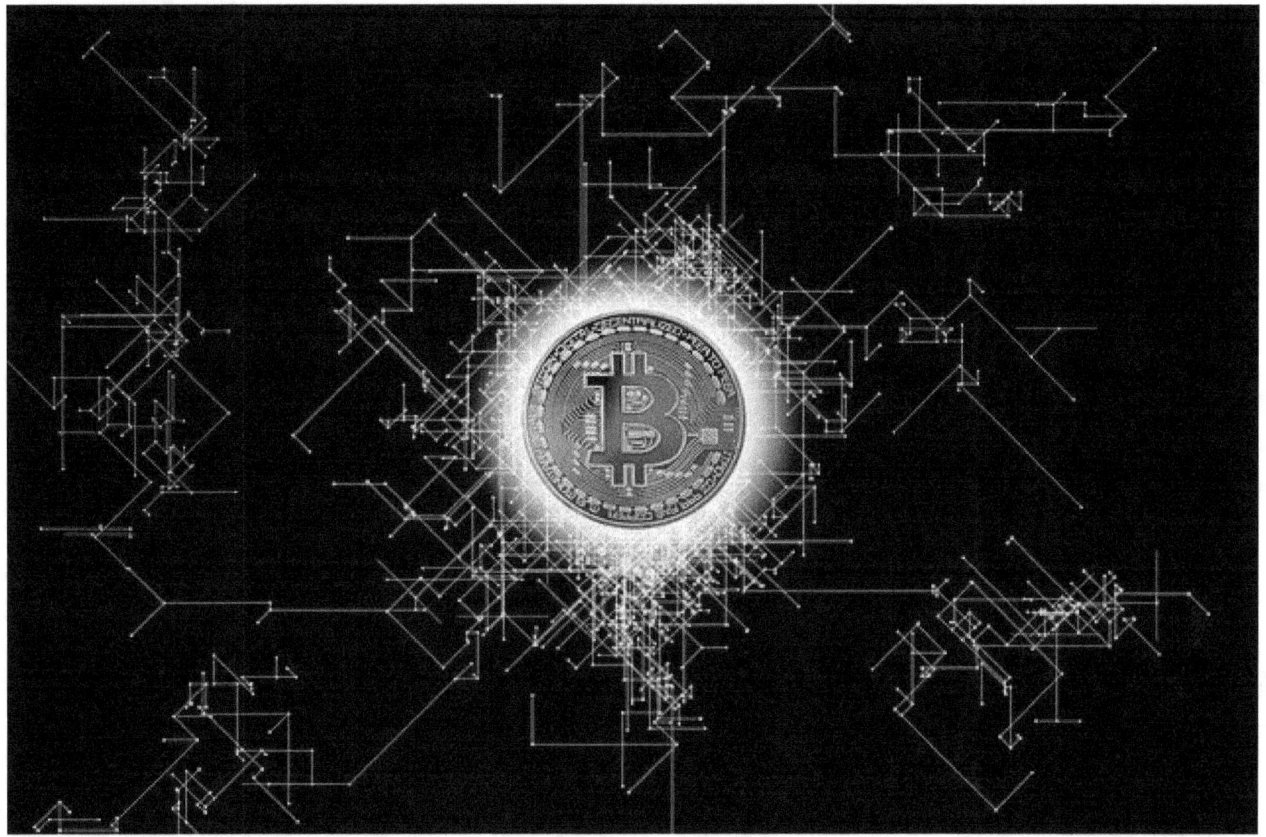

One of the biggest things influencing the volatility of the bitcoin price is its relative anonymity. Unlike traditional exchanges and markets, where the participant data is easily accessible, this virtual money exchange keeps information on each transaction relatively private. All that means is that even if a large number of news stories highlighting potential institutional buy-ins might have increased investor interest, only 1.5 percent of that value added to the price of bitcoin has come from Wall Street, according to Coindesk's index. Financial privacy is one of the main attractions for most traders and investors interested in trading or investing in digital currencies.

The total number of transactions during a week on average is now in the millions. Transactions can include mining, buying, selling, margin buying and even trading back and forth between different currencies. There are three layers to the bitcoin protocol that facilitate the trade: the bitcoin miners, the software developers who write the code, and individual buyers and sellers. Because it operates twenty-four hours a day around the globe, the potential to trade BTC as a currency pair (eg. BTCUSD) simultaneously is great, but the inability of regulators to intervene and influence the price can limit market liquidity.

Because of the lack of real-time information, many people have turned to third-party services to monitor and facilitate their transactions. Services like the major crypto exchanges ensure that there is a sufficient supply of bitcoins to meet the demand by constantly monitoring the market and performing mathematical filters that filter out unsold and oversold units.

Another reason that some investors have chosen not to trade in bitcoin but other cryptos is the volatility of the market. The difficulty of tracking the value of your virtual assets is compounded by the inability to buy or sell them unless you use the right software. One of the reasons that traders feel comfortable trading in the broader altcoin trading market is the freedom of choice that it affords. Although privacy is a feature that some people appreciate in utilizing a decentralized system for trade, others decry it as leaving the door wide open for corporate influence.

In addition to concerns about privacy and influence, a worry that many investors have is the potential return on investment that goes unmatched by any other form of virtual money. Even though the volatility of the market has reduced the per-share earnings of some of the world's biggest corporations, the bitcoin network continues to expand at a daily rate that would easily match those of corporate equity. Despite recent gains in value, the overall trend of the value has been to steadily increase in both volume and price, securing itself as the premier investment fund over the long term. This provides an excellent opportunity for investors to enter the market at a low cost while maximizing returns. While this may be the ideal situation, for individuals interested in securing their wealth, there are several options that can be used to accomplish this.

A key distinction between currencies used in the traditional stock market and those used in the bitcoin ecosystem is the number of units that can be bought or sold. Unlike stocks, which are traded on a single exchange-trading floor, most cryptocurrencies are decentralized and traded throughout the internet. This increases liquidity but also makes it more difficult to accurately pinpoint an overall value for each type of coin. For instance, if the value of a particular major cryptocurrency were to fluctuate dramatically, the individual investor would not be able to execute a successful trade as the entire market would be affected. Because of this, many traders prefer to purchase smaller amounts of a particular cryptocurrency with the hopes that it will increase in value over time as the rest of the market fluctuates.

As with any other investment, there are risks associated with investing in anything that does not have complete trust in the entity that funds it. Satoshi Nakamoto released the bitcoin protocol in 2009 as an open-source solution to this problem. His solution was to create a peer-to-peer software program that was installed on computers around the world that digitally maintained a ledger of all transactions made in the system. Because of this ledger, the network grew and because it was open to anyone with legitimate access, it gained momentum. Today, the network is the backbone of all exchanges operating under the auspices of the bitcoin marketplace.

Transaction fees are also important, and must not be overlooked. While this might seem relatively small, the size of the transaction fees required to facilitate the network has an impact on how the rest of the industry operates. Most online businesses do not accept any currencies other than the US dollar, and because of this, they must pay significant transaction fees to ensure every transaction goes through when their customers want to pay for goods and services in Bitcoin. The high transaction fees also mean that only a small percentage of all buyers and sellers enter the exchange, limiting the amount of money that can change hands. In the event that fees should rise, however, it is possible for users to decrease their activity on the network, creating an environment in which everyone loses out. If this occurs too often, perhaps there could be some altcoins willing to step in and resolve this problem.

Chapter 5 - How Is the Supply of Bitcoins Selected?

Even if you know the basics, you may still have a difficult time relating to the world of bitcoins and how they work. While you may have heard of cryptocurrencies before, you may not understand how this particular form of money works. It's not essential to get too technical about it, but it will likely make things easier for you. This chapter will attempt to give you an understanding of how this type of money works.

As you probably already know, there are two major types of transactions that take place with bitcoin, and one of these is called "blockchain". The word "blockchain" simply refers to the system by which all transactions are recorded. In the simplest of terms, it means that every transaction that is made is entered into a digital record known as the "blockchain". It is this particular record that acts as a ledger of all transactions that have taken place.

Now, since there are two main functions for the bitcoin mining process, you should understand each of them. Here are the two main roles that are served by miners in the bitcoin mining process:

First, miners work to increase the capacity of the bitcoin network, which is called "proof of work". This is important because, without the proof of work, the network cannot function. To ensure that no one monopolizes the process of creating new bitcoins, miners must increase the rate at which they work to add new blocks of transactions to the network. It is at this point in the transaction that new bitcoins are created. Therefore, the process is referred to as "cryptographic miners".

Secondly, the developers of the bitcoin protocol have a large role to play in keeping the chain of transactions running. They do this by adding new features and eliminating bugs that may be present in the code. For example, if there was ever a bug that resulted in an unlimited number of bitcoins being produced, the developer of the bitcoin protocol would fix the bug and then continue to work on it until the fix was made official. At this point in time, the bitcoins used were called "digital cash" and no longer could be traced or owned by anyone else. The process that makes digital cash exist is called "proof of stake".

One of the most commonly referred to features of the bitcoin ecosystem is the bitcoin wallet. A wallet is what you use to store your private key information that is required to transact with the bitcoin network. Your private key information consists of your name, address, private fingerprint, and the number of bitcoins that you desire to transfer from your wallet. The wallet is the place where you hold the keys to your digital currency. Any activity that you perform with the bitcoins should be encrypted.

Unlike more traditional forms of currencies, such as the US dollar, the value of bitcoins is not tied to a single economic factor. Instead, the value of a particular bitcoin is determined by the demand for it among users throughout the world. As a result, there is no central bank controlling the supply of bitcoins, which acts as a safety precaution in case there are instances of misuse. In the case of the US dollar, the government controls the supply because the value is printed in currency. However, when you exchange one type of currency for another, such as the US dollar for Australian dollars, the government is always able to intervene to influence the supply of money in the market.

One of the most important things that a user needs to know about the bitcoin ecosystem is how the supply of bitcoins is set up. The supply is set up so that someone called a miner, controls a certain number of bitcoins. Every 10 minutes a new block of transactions is sent to the network by all miners. Once a transaction has been received by all miners, then it will be added into the "chain", or distributed across the network until it is reviewed and approved.

So, technically, all transactions are made with a specific set of parameters. First, the buyer (the person initiating the sale) must sign off on the sale with a key and then send in the payment. Then, the buyer (the person paying for the goods) signs off and the transaction is considered to have been authorized. The seller (who is the one receiving the goods) similarly signs off and gives an authorization code to the miner. At this point, the miner then verifies the signature on the transaction (which is controlled by the purchaser) and then adds the transaction into the "chain" or spreads the transaction across the network. Because blocks contain large amounts of bitcoin, distribution of fractions of the block are then sent through the network to the correct destination bitcoin wallets.

PART 3 – THE ALTCOINS

In this section, let's go into some detail on the the alternative cryptocurrencies and we'll find out if any of them can someday contend for the Bitcoin crown as King of Cryptos. Let's get into some details on the altcoins contending with the Bitcoin King.

Chapter 6 - Meet The Contenders

The most important altcoins we will discuss are the top 15 cryptocurrencies on coinmarketcap.com as of date of this publication. These includes 3 coins that are US dollar backed cryptocurrencies.

So here they are...

These are the most promising cryptocurrencies that can compete with and maybe someday surpass Bitcoin in overall market capitalization:

Ethereum (ETH)

Cardano (ADA)

Binance Coin (BNB)

US Dollar backed cryptos: Tether (USDT), USD Coin (USDC) and Binance USD (BUSD)

Ripple (XRP)

Dogecoin (DOGE)

Polkadot (DOT)

Solana (SOL)

Uniswap (UNI)

Bitcoin Cash (BCH)

Litecoin (LTC)

Chainlink (LINK)

Chapter 7 - The Vitality Of The Ethereum Smart Contract

If you are wondering what exactly Ethereum is and what value can it give you, then read through this current chapter closely. Firstly, an Ethereum is a distributed ledger utilizing smart contracts to facilitate instant transfers of funds. In contrast to conventional blockchains like Bitcoins, which have block sizes of around one megabyte each, an Ethereum will have a much higher maximum size per block. But in essence, the purpose of using this particular technology is to replace the traditional blockchains, which by now are seriously lacking in terms of scalability.

Secondly, an Ethereum will allow its users to run a Smart Contract on top of the main chain. This Smart Contract will allow users to transact without requiring the mediation of a third party. So ethereum, being an open-source protocol and therefore free for anyone to use, will also be perfect for developers. The developers will be able to easily create custom blockchains as their wish.

Thirdly, when you talk about Ethereum, you should know that it provides developers a way to create and publish their smart contracts, thereby giving them ultimate control of the transactions. In contrast to other blockchains like Bitcoin and Litecoin, there will be no third party involved in any transaction that is made on Ethereum. The only time there will be a third party is when someone submits a new transaction.

Once again, we will be discussing the benefits of the ethereum network. Developers will be able to freely develop their own applications on top of this highly advanced platform. They can also publish their own applications on the ethereum main net. When this is done, the smart contract or the programming code will be executed in real-time without any delays whatsoever. With such a feature, any type of business will have the ability to utilize its applications to earn income, while at the same time, being protected against any losses. With all these benefits, we can say that the use of Ethereum is something great.

What's more, with the use of the ethereum along with the other upcoming applications of the Ethereum smart contracts, the future for decentralized apps will certainly brighten. Now, every company or organization will no longer need to depend on the companies that are providing the services via the traditional servers and platforms. Now, these companies can simply provide the necessary services via the ethereum platform. They can also offer their users the ability to communicate using the most popular social media channels via their smart contracts.

Moreover, with the Ethereum technology, there will also be fewer chances of delays in the transactions. This is because it will run based on the soon-to-be widely used proof-of-stake algorithm. In this manner, the chances of having a successful transaction are higher. Another benefit that we can get from the use of the Ethereum smart contract is that users will be able to enjoy instant updates. This is because they will be able to transact their transactions through their social media accounts.

The recent developments in the field of Ethereum have indeed proven to be very promising. There are a lot of reasons why developers and entrepreneurs are now taking advantage of the benefits that the Ethereum has to offer. As a matter of fact, there are more than a few developers who have already begun operating their businesses using the Ethereum smart contracts. This is a clear indication that there are still things that the ethereum project needs to make progress on.

Furthermore, as long as ethereum gains more popularity among the different developers and entrepreneurs, we can expect that there will be more exciting and beneficial developments in the future.

Chapter 8 - Why Invest in in the Ethereum token, ERC20?

There's no denying that the hype behind ethereum and its ERC20 token has reached a fever pitch recently. The mere mention of its name brings to mind a world where the internet, financial markets, and technology converge. Everyone seems to be talking about it - investors, developers, industry leaders, even government officials, all seem to be on the lookout for the ethereum revolution. But what is ethereum, how does it work, and what are its uses? Following continues our discussion of the crypto coin that aims to put an end to the problems plaguing the traditional money transfer mechanism.

An anonymous currency that combines different elements of distributed computing such as Distributed Ledger Technology (DLT), proof-of-work based proof-of computational authority (POW tokens), and smart contracts between individuals may sound like a complicated idea. However, the coins combine the best aspects of several of these elements into one efficient, and highly scalable payment protocol. In other words, ether is a unique combination of currencies that are based on the open-source programming code that goes into the popular decentralized Internet technologies like Distributed Ledger Technology (DET) and Proof-of Computing. On top of that, ethereum's flexible design enables the use of multiple languages and the integration of blockchains. The combination of these three factors makes it one of the most appealing forms of decentralized technologies.

One of the biggest attractions of ether is that it makes it easy for users to transact in real-time. In other words, the protocol makes instant payments possible. Through smart contracts, users can specify exactly what they want their money to do - from security fees to withdrawal. The smart contracts also define the rules for when certain tokens are allowed to be withdrawn. Since ethereum network transactions are executed peer to peer, this ability to transact instantly is very valuable.

However, not all apps can run on ethereum. Since ethereum is new and still in the development stages, many developers have yet to create an official e Ethereum wallet and/or ethereum compatible browser. While this may seem like a disadvantage, because ethereum is still relatively new there will be a huge demand for developers creating these apps. Therefore, by having a web browser that uses ethereum you will be able to purchase ether using ether tokens which are identical to the traditional online currency.

As mentioned before, another attraction of ethereum is that it is fully compatible with the widest variety of wallets, whether they be for desktop mobile or web. Since ethereum's distributed ledger is more advanced than that of other leading cryptocurrencies, its native mobile apps are expected to be some of the most cutting edge in terms of smartphone technology. This is an especially attractive proposition for enterprises that need to conduct corporate finance transactions on the go. Even if you don't need a mobile app for ether, the opportunity to participate in the wider global network of enthusiasts for the protocol should provide you with another strong reason to buy ether and participate in the future growth of ethereum. The very same characteristics that make ethereum so appealing to a wide variety of investors and entrepreneurs make it ripe for a successful Initial Coin Offerings (ICO) campaign.

The bright future that awaits ether means that the network that supports it will continue to expand its roster of clients. While the present roster currently includes some prominent venture capital and private equity firms, there is no doubt that the roster is always going to grow as the world becomes more familiar with the protocol and its open-source platform. If you have any reservations about investing in new technology like this one then the best advice would be to wait another few months. In the meantime, you can invest in other currencies and projects that have a better track record for being successful in the future.

One final advantage to buying an ethereum smart contract is that you can use the proceeds from your investment to buy additional tokens and increase the value of your portfolio even faster than you could with traditional methods of investing. Unlike stocks and bonds, which can take years to return a profit, your profits from investments on the ethereum platform occur in a matter of weeks. You can see the benefit of this by thinking about all of the money you will save throughout your career. However, remember these markets are highly volatile and, depending upon your risk tolerance and leverage, can make you a lot of money in short periods or make you lose money if your timing is off. For this reason, leverage trading is not recommended for beginners because even though the upside is greater, the risk itself is also much greater. As we'll discuss later in this book, dollar-cost averaging may be the optimal strategy for investing in cryptos like ethereum.

These are only a few reasons why you should be excited about investing in the future of ethics and cryptography. The developers of ether have taken the protocol one step closer to becoming an open-source protocol that anyone interested in disrupting the existing order set up in the financial industry can take advantage of. With ether being among the most modern crypto technology platforms available, the future for crypto networks like ethereum looks promising indeed.

Chapter 9 - What Is Cardano?

Cardano (ADA) is described as a privacy coin. It is an open-source protocol aiming to improve on the lessons learned from the bitcoin and ethereum protocols. It was created by experts in the field of computer science, cryptography, and finance. They believe that it has many advantages over other forms of currencies, most notably the traditional coins in circulation. It was created to complement other currencies that are currently out there.

Unlike other coins, Cardano is designed to run on its decentralized network. Unlike previous coins that depend on central banks for their issuance, Cardano relies on individual entities called nodes. These nodes form the network that makes up the entire network of Cardano. Transactions are performed through the use of smart contracts that are programmed into the digital currency's code. Because this feature is unique among privacy coins, many refer to it as being the most private form of currency in existence.

A major selling point of Cardano, as well as the reason why it's quickly gaining in popularity, is that the platform is completely free of charge. Unlike most other coins, which have high gas fees that can cripple a business's bottom line, Cardano allows you to use the network for free. The network, also known as the "cardio" platform, sends transactions without the need for user interaction. This is in contrast to most other platforms, which include a fee for each transaction.

Another selling point for the cardio project is its ability to run on multiple blockchains. By using three separate but cooperating independent servers called "zones," Cardano can run on three different networks. These include the Waves platform, the SBI-e, and the Ledger Platform. All of these networks work together to facilitate Cardano trades, which are conducted in real-time. This feature makes the Cardano project perfect for businesses that may not wish to take on additional capital to operate on their own.

One more selling point that Cardano has been its highly competitive price. Unlike most other ICO platforms, the Cardano project charges a significantly lower amount per trade. Even after the hard work, which could raise the price of the coin, the current exchange rate stands at reasonable prices, well below the average of many competing coins. This price difference is particularly notable in comparison with the overall average of all coins.

However, perhaps the most important selling point for Cardano is how it operates on two different blockchains. On one hand, the token is backed by the pre-mine. On the other hand, the pre-mine is used as collateral for the security of the actual coin. Each side has advantages, depending on how they look at it. Here is how the coin projects work on both chains:

The pre-mine is used as collateral for the execution of the Cardano contract. Specifically, the tokens are controlled by the Cardano Foundation and cannot be fractionalized, i.e. exchanged directly with any person or business. Instead, the Foundation issues a limited number of tokens, and adds them into the first blockchain.

Chapter 10 – Cardano's Advanced Proof Of Stake

Cardano (ADA) is an upcoming digital currency platform. ADA cryptocurrency is being developed by Cardano, the developer of ADA a financial instrument similar to Gemini. Cardano's protocol is expected to combine privacy, scalability, and robustness in the distributed ledger technology space.

ADA cryptocurrency is designed for low-cost smart cards that can be embedded in a wide range of electronic products such as smartphones and medical equipment. This will give access to real-time financial transactions in the form of receipts. As the co-founder and developer of ADA say "ADA is not about currencies, it is about designing the way information flows in the distribution grid of our marketplaces". ADA cryptocurrency will provide a bridge between the second and third-generation platforms.

In contrast to the existing networks such as Visa and MasterCard, Cardano aims to create blocks that are resistant to external factors that may bring about a network failure or any other effect that may degrade the security of the system. Cardano co-founded the Open Ledger Foundation intending to build a censorship-resistant backbone for the entire network. The Foundation is led by Cardano's co-founder, who holds a doctorate degree in Computer Science, specializing in digital currencies.

One of the features of ADA is its Proof of Stake mechanism, which uses a special algorithm to distribute transaction fees among the users of the network. The way this works is simple: users will create blocks on their devices that will serve as evidence that they are financially able to sustain the network. Once approved, these blocks will be checked by a consensus algorithm. This process will prevent the users of the network from generating duplicate content, thereby eliminating the possibility of centralization. In addition, the proof-of-stake function will also allow the users of the currency to generate rewards for being part of the network.

ADA utilizes a new technological advancement that is composed of nodes that receive and forward requests for blocks of transactions to one or more other nodes. Transactions are instant and are covered by multilayered security guarantees that make the transactions secure even when performed on the public marketplace. Since the transactional nature of the blockchains requires that the participants agree to certain terms, ADO uses smart contract technology to ensure that the agreed terms are actually implemented in the real world. Because the distribution of transactions is controlled through the use of smart contracts, there is virtually no possibility of outside interference or manipulation.

Because the Cardano protocol enables users of the network to generate rewards for the production of new blocks of transactions, the Cardano smart contracts do not need to be centrally administered. Because the Cardano protocol validates the validity of each transaction in the form of a proof-of-stake, no third party is needed to control or monitor Cardano. With the Cardano backend using a tamper-resistant digital signature program, complete decentralization of administration is possible, allowing users to freely choose which software programs they run and which they don't.

Because the Cardano software program is based on new innovative technology, it is believed to be the first true app that uses the breakthrough called homesteading. The homesteading concept states that the tokens generated by the Cardano ecosystem can be used voluntarily. In other words, you are not forced to invest in the Cardano platform if you don't want to. This gives users of the decentralized apps the freedom to decide on what they feel comfortable investing in.

At this point, it is unclear how far Cardano has to go. Currently, it appears that the team behind the project is working to build upon the already impressive technological foundation that is Cardano. However, for the project to take off and become a true competitor to the likes of Bitcoin and Ethereum, it will have to overcome some significant obstacles. One such hurdle is the fact that the token base is still in the experimental stages. However, the future certainly looks bright for Cardano.

Chapter 11 - What Are Stablecoins?

Stablecoins are an asset class of digital asset that has asset values that are based solely on the performance of the US dollar. Three of the most important stable coins backed by USD are discussed in this book including Tether (USDT), USD Coin (USDC), and Binance USD (BUSD).

That is not to say that all the coins on the Binance smart chain are backed by the US dollar. No, that is not the case. What this means is that when you purchase a stable coin on the Binance exchange, you are purchasing a product that is backed in whole or in part by the US dollar. Once you make a purchase you will receive a quote of the cost of this asset-based upon its current spot price. At that point, you have that asset secured in US dollars.

The other thing that is different about this asset class is that you do not have a "use it or lose it" guarantee attached to them. What this means is that your purchase of stablecoins on the Binance exchange is not a loan. Your ability to sell your stable coins is unlikely to be impacted significantly should the marketplace take a turn for the worse (which it sometimes does) is limited. This is not the case with other virtual currencies on the market. That being said, the costs and risks associated with stablecoins are quite different than those associated with other types of altcoins.

For example, when Binance works their customers' assets (stored in US Dollars) through the Binance stablecoins process, it is equivalent to a loan. It is very similar to what is done with unsecured debt on the banking industry. Once the customer makes his payments, he is typically asked not to spend the money but instead be given a check for his payment. With stablecoins, the customer can purchase as many coins as he wants until his balance hits a pre-determined maximum.

Since bitcoins and ethereum are not backed by fiat currency in any way, their value is strictly determined by market movements in the markets they are traded in. As a result, you can't know for sure if you will see a profit from your purchase, especially if you are a short term trader. The same can be said for all other altcoins that are not stablecoins. The former are all based on speculation and risk management and do not guarantee any form of liquidity. The difference is that stablecoins users enjoy price stability, whereas in most other types of crytocurrency prices tend to vary widely.

Unlike most other altcoins, stablecoins are issued through the use of an "interbank" system instead of through private lending institutions. Private lending institutions are subject to strict regulations from the US Federal Government in terms of their interest rates and the amount they can lend. Because of this, there is very little leeway allowed to brokers and the general public in terms of the amount they can lend. These institutions are required to follow strict guidelines and are heavily regulated. This means that stablecoins can be much more secure and reliable, leading to a long list of benefits when using them.

There are several other advantages to using stablecoins, but these are the two biggest benefits that all investors should be aware of. These listings include stable Cryptocurrency markets, high liquidity, and long-term value ties to fiat US dollars. All of these features work hand-in-hand to provide long-term profits to investors who make the right choices when using stablecoins to invest in other crypto assets. The list of stable coins offered by the exchanges continues to grow as more investors discover its advantages.

Chapter 12 - Which Are the Best Stablecoins?

Stablecoins have emerged as a stable replacement for traditional methods of investment such as certificates of deposit (CDs), individual savings accounts (ESAs), and even money market mutual funds and stocks. These stable cryptosystems offer a flexible investment option for both businesses and individuals while providing an unparalleled level of safety. Stable coins are often referred to as tethers, stable money, or tethers. A stable coin will not lose value just as gold does, and it is usually easy and quick to sell if the market needs to move in a negative direction. This type of investment provides a low risk with a large potential for high returns.

Several investors are attracted by the promise of safe returns with high liquidity and easy management. As discussed above, this asset class involves a digital asset that is traded on the Internet between two parties. The benefit of this is the quick transfer of funds, and there are many different types of stable coins including gold and silver backed stablecoins, precious metals backed stablecoins, and commodities backed stablecoins. Although this asset class attracts many different types of investors, two types are especially appealing to new investors. These include the gold and silver-backed stablecoins, and the precious metals and commodities-backed stablecoins.

Gold and silver-backed stablecoins are very attractive to investors due to their stability. Unlike gold and silver, the price of stablecoins does not fluctuate as much. Generally, stablecoins that are backed by precious metals are considered to be quite secure since physical possession is necessary to guarantee their value. This type of stability is attractive to investors who need a steady source of income but are not interested in putting too much of their assets at risk.

Another type of stablecoins that is appealing to several different types of investors is the precious metals and commodities backed secure Coins. Since this market is much more volatile than the gold and silver market, it is best to diversify one's investments to ensure the best returns. In addition to the gold and silver-backed secure coins, this market also features a wide range of other coins such as Eurozone Notes, Chinese Panda Coins, and South African Krugerrand Coins. Investing in this kind of stablecoins is a great way to improve one's portfolio since it is less risky than investing in gold or silver.

Several different countries back these stablecoins. In the past, stablecoins were backed by the U.S. dollar. Currently, several governments, both international and national, are backing the currency. For example, the Canadian government offers to back for their version of the Canadian Maple Leaf. Other common countries backing stablecoins include Switzerland, the Netherlands, Italy, and the United Kingdom.

Many investors are attracted to investing in these stablecoins because they offer a relatively safe investment vehicle. While there are certain risks associated with investing in any form of fiat currency, the benefits far outweigh the risks when it comes to stablecoins. One major benefit is that since they are backed by a national currency, investors can be confident that their investment will retain its value even in difficult economic times. This is not the case for many other types of currencies, which often lose value due to political instability or financial crises. With the unstable economic conditions throughout the world, investors often fear that their investment will lose its worth, which causes them to liquidate their holdings.

Another benefit of investing in stablecoins is the low premiums compared to other forms of investment. Since the cost of maintaining a fiat currency is relatively high, many investors are taking advantage of this fact by investing in stablecoins. This is particularly true for investors who have a large amount of capital, which they would otherwise use to back up their fiat currency. For example, during a recent economic crisis, it was financially prudent for European investors to invest in U.S. dollars instead of relying on their domestic currency.

To find out which are the best stablecoins right now, it is important to examine both the benefits and the risks associated with them. By closely examining these two factors, you will be able to determine if investing in this form of alternative investment is right for you. After you have decided to purchase stablecoins, you will need to learn how to get started. There are many ways to acquire this important asset, but the easiest method is by utilizing what is known as a "BTC tether" also called BTCUSDT. By using a BTC tether, you can access the most diverse collection of stablecoins, which will enable you to begin to profit from this exciting new way of investing in the digital landscape.

Chapter 13 - Trading Stablecoins

In addition to fiat currency-backed stable coins, there are new stable coin groups of digital currencies that are backed by some commodity, which attempts to provide long-term price stability. The object of stablecoins is to provide a medium for trading between different buyers and sellers that attempt to make long-term investment decisions without worrying about the potential volatility of any particular currency. Stable coins have recently gained traction as they strive to provide the most of both worlds i.e. the speed of instant transaction processing and the maximum privacy and protection of transactions of other currencies.

There are two major categories of stablecoins that are used by most traders. The first is the Money Trust (MTT), which is issued by the government of the United States as a legal tender and is a legal international currency used in Forex Trading. The US government guarantees the availability of this financial instrument, although the list of other countries may expand in the future.

The second major stable coin group is the peg Digital Currency (FCX), which is issued by the Swiss National Bank. FCX is NOT a physical coin but a virtual currency in the form of a redeemable debit card. This card is linked to the Eurozone banking system and offers users the ability to purchase Eurozone securities and carry out transactions in the same way as if they were conducting a trade themselves.

Although there are several forms of stablecoins being traded, it is difficult to compare them to any other asset such as stocks or bonds because no physical asset exists that can be converted instantaneously into a digital asset like a currency. StableCoins are a decentralized form of money that has not been determined by any central governing body and their value derives solely from their peg to fiat or commodity as well as the demand and supply in the market to a limited extent.

Since its launch, there have been millions of trades made using stablecoins. The stablecoins can also be a digital version of precious metals such as gold and silver, and they act like traditional precious metals. However, instead of holding the metal in a form of bullion or coins, investors usually buy them as smart contracts with the central bank of the country where they are deposited.

When the investor decides to sell his shares, he can do so by sending a request to the central bank, who then hands over the coin to the buyer.

Chapter 14 - Tether Currency and Commodity Indexes Can Be Investment Bridges For Crypto Investors

Tether is a stable coin cryptocurrency linked to the US Dollar. Tether (money) is backed by a collateral base, which can be the US Dollar or some other global common currency. Tether can be traded like a futures contract and used as an alternative to the Euro or the Swiss Franc. When tether is linked to the US dollar, it can be abbreviated USDT.

Tether (USDT) is not a typical currency. It is a Cryptocurrency Tether, which is backed by a US reserve asset and therefore is worth one US dollar per token. Tether (money) is not linked to any conventional asset class, such as stocks, bonds, commodities, or the like.

The Tether contract awards rights to assets held within a pool of digitally signed ether certificates, which are themselves backed by tethers. These certificates are also distributed to holders according to their entitlement. A holder is someone who is entitled to one or more tethers and is usually referred to as a "peer". Each peer is assigned a commission by Tether to compensate him for his services in generating the ether.

The term "stablecoin" is sometimes used interchangeably with "crypto-tether". A decade ago the term "crypto-tether" was used to describe any type of digital asset that was backed or exchanged by a nontraditional digital asset. This was later extended to include any tradable "crypto-tether", i.e. coins, papers, bonds, warranties, etc. Today the term "crypto-tether" refers to any tradable asset issued on the basis of a "Crypto Currency" (i.e. money) issued by an issuer who is not a traditional bank or by a government or by a centralized issuer acting under the authority of a government.

Tether itself was not launched as a stable coin or even as a hedge against speculative currency exposure. It was launched as a proof of concept by Tether Limited to demonstrate its technology and to attract developers and entrepreneurs to its platform. In hindsight, this was a very clever marketing move because it attracted attention to the lack of a truly secure and profitable tradable product. At the time nobody knew what a secure tradable product could be. Since the issuance of Tether was supposed to act as an anchor in the market, it was only natural that we would want to know exactly what it would be.

There are several problems associated with Fiat Currency in the sense that they are backed up by nothing other than credit card power, and the issuers of such currency rely on nothing but public opinion to continue issuing them. The entire process of issuing them can be rather wasteful and inefficient. This is because it has to be done to keep the price level high enough so that people will buy into the base (the Tether) and then use it as leverage against any increase in the trading volume of the underlying asset which causes the price to rise. So the whole system works on speculation rather than on fundamental merits.

Tether isn't the first new token backed by USD which launched. There have been several, but they have all failed to achieve anything meaningful. The newest token will be different because it is backed by an actual physical commodity - the token will be issued based on gold and silver and will be traded on the FX market. Because there are no speculators involved there will be no more pump and dump scams and there will also be a limited trading volume. This is because everybody knows that there is no place for speculative trading when you are dealing with physical commodities.

Tether is an example of a new service that is being introduced that will hopefully be adopted by other exchanges and perhaps even the conventional money markets. It is something like a bridge between digital asset-backed coins and fiat currencies that are backed by actual commodities like gold and silver. In time this may be a very useful service as a bridge between various forms of trading.

Chapter 15 - Binance Coin: Altcoin Associate With A Crypto Exchange

Binance Coin (BNB) is an alternate currency (altcoin) managed by Binance, a leading online trading company. Binance. Binance offers a high-performance electronic currency trading platform. Binance users can generate BNB as interest from their investments, or use it for paying transaction fees to other traders.

Binance Coin is a highly liquid altcoin, but it's a private marketplace currency that enables you to trade using real money on the global Binance exchange, without having to give away your hard-earned cash. Binance Coin can be traded anonymously through the use of pooled trades, thus increasing the liquidity factor while at the same time decreasing the overall risk.

Binance is considered to be a great investment because it has a low volatile price and relatively low trading volume. Binance coins are not backed by any governmental institutions.

Binance Coins are traded in the same way as any other kind of virtual currency. Smart contract technology allows traders to create a self-executing, automated, real-time trading platform that automates all monetary transactions on the Binance exchange. Binance uses four different types of virtual money: the Binance Cash virtual currency, Binance Gold virtual currency, Binance tokens, and Binance coins. Binance tokens are backed by real tokens (e.g., the Euro) and have no trading fees. This is in contrast to Binance Gold which is backed by actual gold certificates.

Trading fees are applied to each transaction that costs the trader a fee regardless of whether or not the trade is successful. The rate that is applied to Binance trading fees is determined by the volatility factor. This is a complex calculation formula that takes into account the start and end times of the period being evaluated. The purpose of this complicated formula is to determine the market value of the asset for each period during which a Binance Coin is exchanged.

In a nutshell, Binance exchanges are either peer-to-peer (PPC) or futures exchanges based on one or more currencies. A peer-to-peer Binance coin exchange is similar to a stock exchange where trade transactions occur between buyers and sellers. On the other hand, the main difference between a futures exchange and a PPC is that there is no physical product that is held between brokers. Futures exchanges are solely virtual exchanges where traders speculate on future price movements of assets by agreeing to buy or sell a specific quantity of an asset at a future date and agreed price.

There are four types of Binance Coin exchanges; the Binance Coin Market, the Binance OTC Market, the Binance Virtual Cash Markets, and the Binance Mutual Funds. The Binance Coin Market trades the popular altcoins such as Litecoin, Dogecoin, and the popular Binance coin. The Binance OTC Market trades popular virtual currencies such as the US Dollar, the Euro, the Yen, and the Swiss Franc. The Binance Virtual Cash Markets trades popular commodities. Finally, the Binance Mutual Fund is an ETFX that is largely based on stocks and options with financial risk tolerance primarily involving futures and options. Each of these four types of exchanges has different risk profiles that will vary the amount of return that can be realized from each trade.

Binance is an excellent platform for anyone interested in investing in any of the four major cryptosystems currently out there. Binance will allow you to easily analyze the market, find profitable trades, and make profitable trades on your own terms. Binance is one of the first exchange platforms to offer its clients access to the largest and most liquid cryptosystems available. As long as you are willing to invest the time and effort into learning about the markets and becoming familiar with the important altcoins, then Binance should be a good platform for you to use with your investing plans.

Chapter 16 - Binance Smartchain

Binance Coin is a new type of virtual currency established with the Binance Exchange in which a person can trade cryptocurrencies funded by fiat currency money. The purpose of Binance Coin is to help new and private traders who are interested in investing in emerging cryptocurrencies. If you are an investor and would like to learn more about Binance Coin, you will want to keep on reading. In this chapter, you will discover more about Binance Coin and what it can do for you!

Binance Coin is a new type of virtual currency that functions similarly to shares. Binance Coin is issued by Binance, which is a large firm that provides a platform for investors, traders, and institutions to enter into a chain of transactions, known as the smart chain.

Although Binance does not operate with any major central exchange, Binance Coin is still a powerful trading platform. Binance uses three major exchanges. These exchanges provide liquidity and allow for maximum trading volume and security. While these three exchanges do not operate in the same manner as the US dollar or the Euro, the trading volume is comparable.

Binance coins are also referred to as tokens or virtual gifts. To participate in the exchange, you need Binance accounts. Binance accounts are also known as e-Wallet, e Wagering, or OTC wallets.

As for the exchange itself, there are no face-to-face meetings, no broker fees, and no set number of coins that one can buy or sell. In some ways, Binance Coin is just another virtual toy. It is not a tangible asset that you can hold or purchase. There are also no set utility coins that you can exchange as well; this makes Binance very different from the other platforms.

The Binance smartboard is an attraction to investors who have purchased Binance coins as well as anyone planning to invest in the platform. The smartboard offers financial services that include money transfers, deposit and withdrawal services, online account management, and investing options such as smart stocks and smart currencies. By utilizing the smart board, you can convert your Binance coins into virtually any virtual currency in the Binance smart coin ecosystem. With these services, you receive a multitude of benefits that can include instant conversions, high transaction fees, reduced transaction costs, and low trading commissions.

Binance has attracted a great deal of attention because of its unique features, but it is important to realize that it is not a substitute for the US dollar or the Euro. Binance is simply a platform that allows you to trade in the Cryptocurrency industry. When you go to their website, you will see a list of countries where they currently offer the service so that you can choose which one you would like to do business with. At the bottom of the page, you will find a link that will take you to the signup section where you can complete your registration and become a part of the Binance community. The Binance smart chain network has become a very popular way for individuals to convert their Binance tokens into other valuable currencies.

Chapter 17 - Ripple Protocol For Financial Institutions and Investors

Before getting deeper into understanding this brand new internet application, it would be wise to first know what exactly is Ripple. This chapter will help you discover the solution, (no pun intended).

Ripple (XRP) is an Internet protocol that links two networks: a sending network, called the protocol layer, and a receiving network, called the protocol network. The sending network can be either a peer-to-peer network (P2P) or an internet backbone. The protocol layer connects the two networks with a payment channel. This payment channel is a special transaction language that enables the two networks to identify the ownership of a specific asset when it is transferred between their systems. This is what is needed for Ripple to function effectively.

The goal of ripple is to create a more reliable, more convenient, and faster way for people to exchange money while eliminating much of the hassle traditionally associated with such transactions. ripple works by using a digital cash bot (XRP). XRP is assigned to each transaction that occurs on the ripple network. The idea behind this is to create liquidity by allowing people the ability to trade without depending solely on one centralized exchange. To do this, traders can buy and sell directly using their private currencies. Many companies have utilized the concept of decentralized exchanges and this is where ripple comes in.

One of the most successful uses of this new technology is that of an asset owner transferring ownership of a certain asset from his/her wallet to a ripple broker who then transfers the ownership from the wallet to the asset. When I say private currency, this means that the currency in your wallet is yours and not some fake outdated digital asset. This concept has been utilized by hundreds of thousands of different companies. In this way, a financial advisor could make a small profit selling assets and using the proceeds to buy more attractive tokens.

This also means that you don't need to have a large investment account to participate in the asset transfer process. Since you will only be paying out a small percentage of the total value of the token, it doesn't make sense to have to deposit large amounts of money to trade on the market. Also, if the market turns out bad, you won't be losing a large amount of money as you would if the market goes on a wild run. All of these reasons are why most financial institutions are already starting to use ripple for their investing purposes.

In a nutshell, the ripple is the backbone of a tokenized economy. A financial advisor can start buying up domains of common tokens like gold and other metals in the hopes that they will appreciate in the future. Once they have a list of them, they will open separate accounts on ripple currency exchanges. Their aim is to accumulate as many common tokens as possible while locking in a small percent of the transaction price in real-time. Their goal is to leverage the power of their real-time gross settlement payment network.

Many banks are already using ripple as a portion of their transaction processing capabilities. This is because of how it allows them to take advantage of their customers' real-time gross settlements without having to rely on traditional systems, like credit cards. The banks can add a small amount of value to the tokens because they are not required to hold them as assets. They can also use the tokens immediately when they receive them from customers. This process is known as interbank funding as well.

With so many customers sending money internationally, banks need to be able to process large volumes of transactions. This is where the interbank funding process comes into play. With an escrow account, banks can agree upon a certain price for their common tokens and then let ripple handle the conversion process. By using this escrow account, banks don't have to rely on the intervention of the central ledger, which would cause the costs to rise dramatically.

There are several reasons why the distributed ledger protocol, named ripple, is ideal for a money transfer network. First of all, it's more reliable than most current methods of currency exchange due to its system of international consensus. The other nice thing about ripple is that it's completely transparent, so both the sender and receiver of funds can see exactly what transactions are happening. In the future, it's likely that all financial institutions will use the distributed ledger technology for secure and convenient currency transfers.

Chapter 18 - Validation of Transactions on the XRP Market

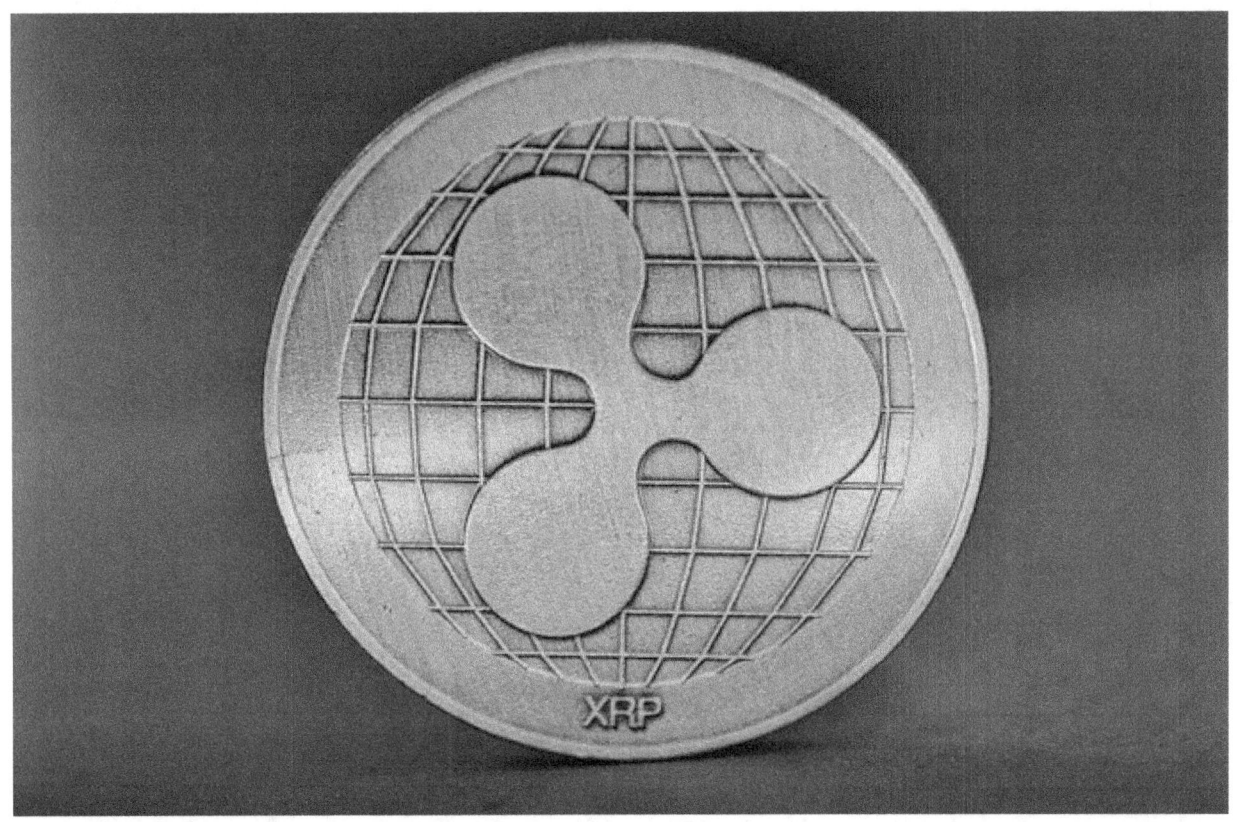

Ripple, (abbreviated as XRP) is an alternative payment protocol (IPC), which is currently undergoing testing. It offers a cost-effective, global settlement method with the potential to reduce transactional costs and boost profitability. In principle, XRP is an unsecured form of digital cash. In contrast to traditional bank-to-bank money transfers, XRP does not use a credit score system and is, therefore, a perfect replacement for credit cards and debit cards. With XRP, there is no need for upfront payments, late fees, and excessive paperwork. Its speed and low cost make it a preferred payment option for most customers.

A digital payment platform, XRP works by allowing its users to convert between currencies using a digital asset, also known as "ripple currency". XRP can be used to transfer funds in place of traditional currencies such as the US dollar, the Euro, the Japanese yen, or the British pound. XRP is traded on major electronic brokers. The Internet has enabled the widespread use of XRP, and it is now used in countries around the world.

The primary goal of XRP is to give retailers and other small business owners an easy way to accept payments from their customers in a matter of minutes. Through this process, merchants will be able to process transactions in real-time, thus eliminating the role of a financial intermediary.

Retail outlets can also benefit from using XRP as a way to attract new customers. Cryptocurrency can be used to build brand recognition and increase exposure. Affiliates can also introduce XRP to their existing clientele, as well as to their potential customers through advertisements and promotions. Through a well-designed advertising campaign, an international money transfer can become almost instant.

Many large financial institutions, including those in the United States and Canada, have been able to successfully process transactions for hundreds of thousands of dollars using Cryptocurrency. The biggest beneficiaries of using XRP for international money transfers are the retailers that use the Digital Product Exchange to enable their customers to make purchases with a local currency. Not only do these retailers benefit from using Cryptocurrency for remittances and other commercial purposes, but they benefit from using the secure Digital Product Exchange as a place to purchase XRP for their businesses.

When the XRP gets converted to Canadian or United States Dollars, the value of the transaction does not change. In the past, when a person wanted to buy an XRP for his/her own business, he/she would need to convert the currency manually into US dollars, since the IRS considers any foreign currency exchanges (including cryptocurrency exchange) as taxable income.

Chapter 19 - Dogecoin: A Boon to Cryptocurrency Investors

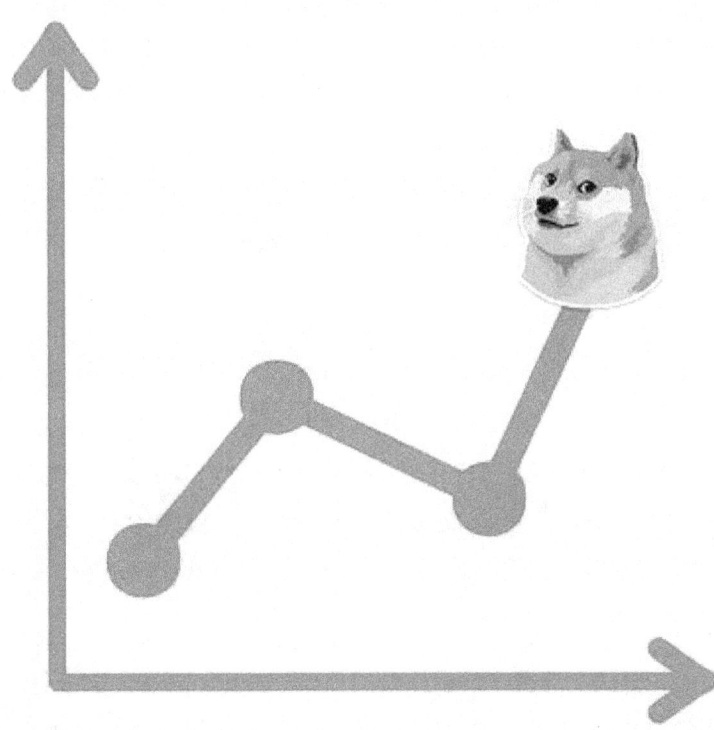

Dogecoin, the digital currency favored by marketers for its low volatility and paltry gains, has taken a beating at times. However, most recently this famous 'meme' coin has been booming. Once considered a joke coin, Dogecoins have been gaining widespread popularity recently.

Several entrepreneurs have taken to creating new Dogeocoins, and several Web sites have popped up offering Dogecoin trading. Some of these new businesses have operated as online scams, others as genuine enterprises aiming to take advantage of the surging popularity of the Dogecoin community. A fourth group, a group calling itself the DOGE Consortium, has issued statements asserting that it is considering ways to replace the existing coins with the newer DOGE currency.

So what is the Dogecoin phenomenon? How did an obscure virtual currency, hardly known outside Internet circles, shoot up in value so quickly? And why are people from places like Silicon Valley lining up to get into the newest

Internet moneymaker? There are several answers to those questions, but they all begin with the idea of a Dogecoin tipping point.

The Dogecoin phenomenon began on April Fools' Day when some anonymous Internet users started promoting the new crypto coin on popular blogging and forum sites. Soon, hundreds of new dogecoins were being traded every hour. Exchanges promptly began popping up, from which traders can buy and sell Dogecoins according to their preference. The frenzy lasted for several weeks until one day a news story reported that a group of high profile Internet personalities had acquired dogecoins worth millions. That's when the whole mess was put into a formal framework known as the Dogecoin memes.

It's easy to see why the Dogecoin memes were such an exciting idea.

But what is Dogecoin? Dogecoin, technically called DOGE, is a form of cryptocurrency that has recently made the news. Dogecoin cards are an offshoot of the original, which featured a special logo designed by an Australian cartoonist. Dogecoin memes use the same format of tweeting as the original tweeters used to make popular posts.

So how does it work? Like many other currencies, Dogecoin uses a finite number of coins to define a certain value. Each transaction is simply divided into one of many possible denominations and is designated with a particular denomination. One of the great advantages to the use of the Dogecoin price as the currency is known for is that it can be used as a barometer for determining the performance of the cryptocoin, namely the strength of its market performance.

For instance, when the Dogecoin price trended upward recently then it was a strong indicator that the market was bullish. Then, when the Dogecoin dropped based on speculative joking comments by Elon Musk, it was a sign of an uptrend had temporarily ended in the marketplace. When the Dogecoin was later again acknowledged by Elon Musk, the coin once again started increasing in value. This was a strong signal that the marketplace was once again trending upwards. The influence that a single individual can have on some low liquidity altcoins is tremendous, and it is a reason that investors should be careful especially in the early days of new cryptocurrencies coming on to the market. However, as the crypto market for each coin matures, the influence of a single individual, including celebrities, will fade. This is because as a cryptocoin such as Doge becomes more popular, its trading volume increases as does its market capitalization. Eventually, as a cryptocoin such as Dogecoin matures, its price should become less volatile over time as the entire marketplace once again determines its actual value.

In summary, Dogecoin has truly broken out in the last few months as one of the major up-and-coming cryptocurrency. Its use as a marketing tool to represent the mood of the cryptocoin has certainly caught the attention of many in the business community.

Chapter 20 - How Dogecoin Marketing Can Improve Its Popularity

DOGE is short for Dog Cash, and although there are certainly some smart investors out there who know about it, many are still unfamiliar. It was created by programmers just for fun, creating an alternative payment method as an ironic joke. Despite its serious comedy tone, some are starting to consider it a legitimate online investment opportunity.

What is DOGE? Dogecoin is an open-source protocol and digital asset designed for the Internet. It can be defined as "a peer-to-peer virtual currency that eliminates the need for actual cash transactions". If you're interested in learning more about this interesting altcoin, please read on. Dogecoin's founders describe it as "the world's first virtual money". It is used as a Meme coin, a novelty that has grown considerably in popularity over the past year or two.

As previously mentioned, DOGE is a peer-to-peer virtual currency that eliminates the need for actual cash transactions. This makes it different from most other existing Altcoins, which often use a Proof-of-work (POW) system to provide proof that a transaction actually took place. By eliminating the need for investing in mining for coins, it makes the process completely transparent and free of any chargebacks.

So what makes DOGE stand out from other existing Altcoins? Its developers created a new mascot for the altcoin that bears a resemblance to the face of an animated doggie from an animated children's TV show. The doggie is the inspiration for the original mascot for the currency The reason for this is that the pair of pink and black dogs are both associated with trendy street styles, and the hyped-up valuation of the cryptocoins make it a prime target for a lot of bloggers and social media users who want to make some quick money.

The founders of dogecoin also created the image of Brains. They aimed to create an image that would be associated with smart digital currencies. The mascot's head resembles that of a human, with the face being a druggie. A ponytail is usually wrapped around his neck and back. His eyes are bright green, signifying the color of the currency. His tail looks like a black duffle bag, representing the lack of value associated with the cryptocoin.

The real value of DOGE is not its image, as it was originally designed to be a lighthearted joke. The real value of this altcoin comes from its low market value. This makes it easy for people to buy it and sell it on popular social media platforms because it is not yet accepted by most merchants. This makes it a perfect "safe" investment as there is no financial risk associated with it.

Due to its low market value, it has not been able to gain much traction. It also lacks the advertising prowess of many other cryptosystems. However, dogecoin investors do not need to worry about the lack of marketing as they can use clever marketing tactics to boost interest in the cryptocoin. One method is to offer giveaway items such as doges, lanyards, and wristbands. These items will have a large circulation in the communities, especially if they are popular and well-received. The more exposure the dogecoin receives, the more it is perceived to increase in value and its worth will rise.

The lack of advertising does not mean that DOGE will not have an effect on the value of bitcoin. The presence of a new cryptocoin increases the liquidity of the market, especially when one considers that there are several competing currencies. Also, dogecoin and bitcoins have a lot in common. Both bitcoins and dogecoins are used as payment in online casinos and their popularity continues to grow. Since it is still relatively new, it will be interesting to see how it fares against the other two competing coins in the future.

Chapter 21- Why Buy Polkadot?

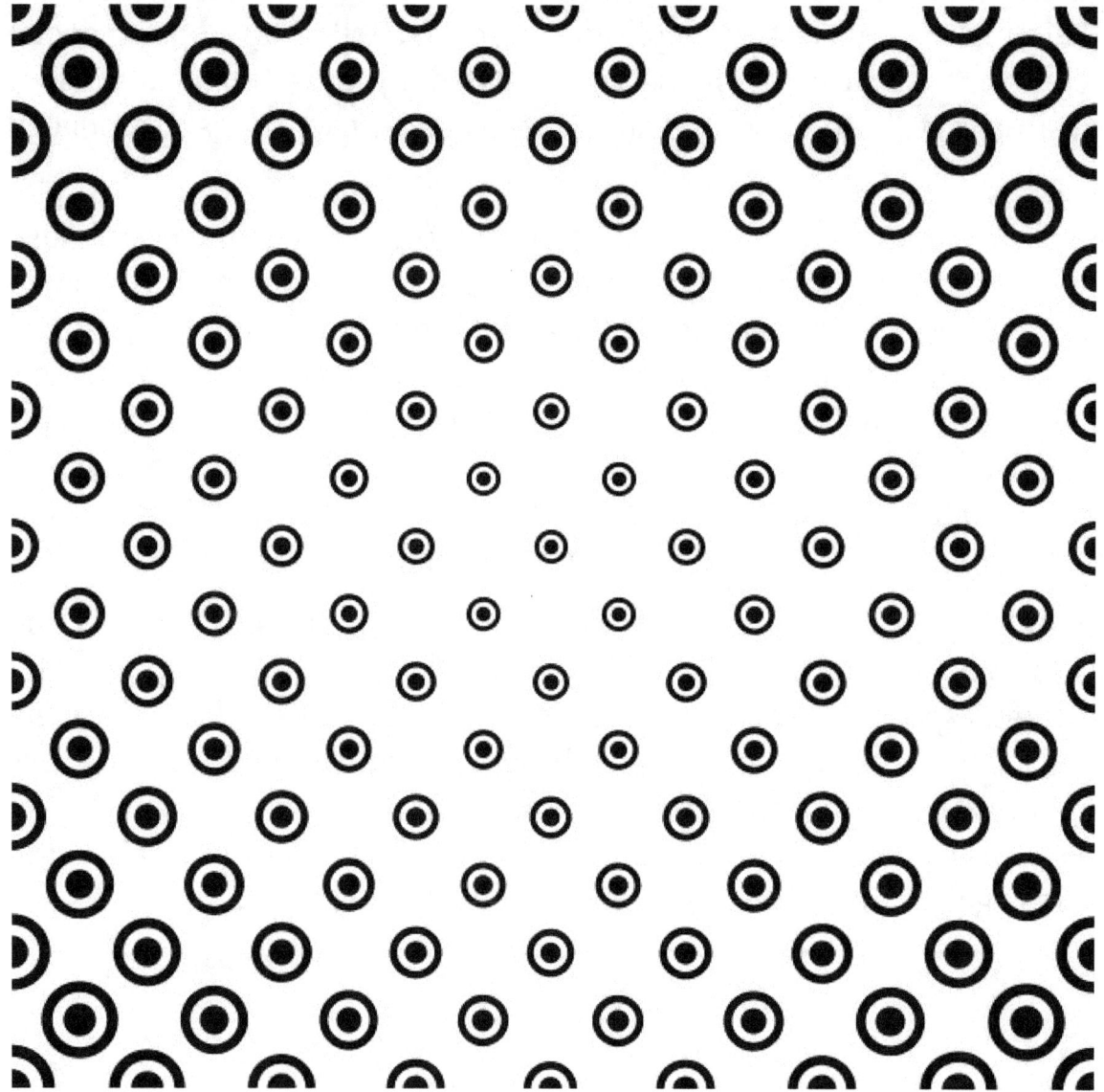

Polkadot is designed to create an automated Internet payment system for the cloud. Polkadot is an open shared heterogeneous multi-tier architecture that allows multiple customized layer one and two "Paradigms" to connect, creating a cloud-native internet of blockchains. The network functions with a proof of stake (POS) based consensus algorithm. The POS is enabled by the use of the Data Channel, which is a bidirectional data channel protocol. It consists of a bidirectional interconnect, gateways, and storage.

Polkadot was developed on the Ethereum protocol as a solution provider in the open-source community. The founders' mission is to build open-source software for the web, ranging from systems for application servers, to database management, to the networking fabric itself. Polkadot has been in development since 2017.

Some key features of Polkadot include the Relay Chain, Parachains, Parathreads, and Bridges. The Relay Chain is in charge of the network's shared security and cross-chain interoperability. Parachains are independent blockchains that can have their tokens running on the Polkadot network. Parathreads are similar to parachains but use a pay-as-you-go model. Finally, Bridges are critical for allowing parathreads and parachains to communicate with outside networks like Bitcoin and Ethereum.

Polkadot was launched with a tokenization system that included several different token types. These tokens are all validators of ownership on the network. At launch, five out of seven protocols, each with a distinct color meaning one of seven things, were supported. At present, Polkadot token usage has grown and is now offered in addition to the original seven token types.

Polkadot offers a scalability option. This scalability is an add-on feature. This feature is referred to as "metacoin." Metacoin is designed to be significantly more robust than other comparable tokens, including Polkadot.

Metacoin was developed as a solution to the problems inherent in decentralized cryptocurrencies. Polkadot's design is to enable token holders to increase their ability to influence the market by allowing them to control more of the total supply of tokens. By adding a scalability option to the Polkadot token, it is believed it will increase its market cap. The increase in market cap will, in turn, increase liquidity, which will help the liquidity gap between investors and capital markets.

It's likely the increase in market cap will also lead to increased diversity of supply and demand. This will create volatility in the pricing of Polkadot. It will also create greater room for the developers of these new cryptocurrencies built on Polkadot to specify new protocol rules. This will allow them to continue refining the underlying asset base while meeting their deadlines. As developers continue to meet their deadlines, it is likely that interest in decentralized cryptocoins like Polkadot will increase. This will create an environment in which developers will be less concerned about technical issues, and more worried about building a strong community around the project.

The ability to change staking formulas will play a large role in the long-term success of Polkadot. The ability to quickly adapt to new staking methods will give Cryptocurrency traders the confidence to trade with lower risks and potentially bigger profits. While many current ICO networks are not adapting to the new demands of modern investors, it seems that Polkadot has the potential to become a leader in the emerging field of crypto portfolios. Due to the large staking percentage required to launch a successful ICO fundraiser, the price of Polkadot will likely remain competitive for the next several years.

This is one of the reasons investors will be attracted to invest in the company's existing chains. However, they may also want to add Polkadot to their portfolio because of the inherent value and security afforded by the technology. Even before its launch in 2017, Polkadot had been making great strides. With over $90k invested during the first week and increasing consistently since then, Polkadot founders easily achieved their goal of having 100% pre-ICO financing. And for several years now since its launch, Polkadot has been showing tremendous potential in offering a revolutionary blockchain with a consistently increasing market cap. This shows that investors see the great potential of buying Polkadot for co-development with the goal of making the technology available to the chains they already own or intend to acquire.

Chapter 22 - Solana Core Developers - Discusses How They Made a Difference With Their Proof of Stake Model

The SaaS ecosystem is growing rapidly. Companies such as Microsoft, Salesforce, Apple, and IBM have created their cloud services. Since then, there has been much talk about how to scale a SaaS platform. scalability refers to the ability to add more users and resources without requiring drastic changes to business models. Solana aims to address these shortcomings without compromising decentralization or security.

Launched in March 2020 by Solana Labs, the Solana ecosystem projects a new approach to verifying online transactions. The goal of the platform is to provide buyers and sellers with the ability to transact over the internet in real-time with minimal overhead for both parties. Many other projects suffer from high scalability issues and slow speeds. While this solution may not provide an ideal environment for real-time data transfers, it does offer promise in the form of lower cost and higher performance during peak times.

To enable buyers and sellers to transact on the network, each participant must create a digital asset that acts as a unique digital key. Transactions are validated via a Distributed Ledger Interface (DLI). The Validator component of solar provides a bridge between the buyers and sellers and validates the transactions performed by each respective participant. The Validator serves as an intermediary and validates all transactions against a set of digital certificates stored on the ledger. The certificates maintain cryptographically secured proof that the transactions conducted by each participant are legal and fair under the current laws of the network. Each certificate carries a link back to the originating Distributed Ledger Interface (DFI).

The proof generated by each validator is stored in the ledger, making it possible for the ledger to act as a Byzantine consensus mechanism. By creating several independent, unique keys, each participant can prove the legality and fairness of each transaction. As each proof builds up in the ledger, users gain complete control over their money and their private information. Once a sufficient number of validators are connected, the ledger itself proves the validity and consistency of all transactions and forms a trustworthy foundation for the entire system. This is the basis of Solana.

The proof/stake methodology of slang differs from that of most blockchains. Staking is a concept inherent in blockchains since they work to keep transaction costs low. By placing a percentage of the total amount of coins in a stake or collateral group, users ensure that their transaction fees are enforced and that their stake is protected in case of a failure. By contrast, the proof/stake methodology creates a baseline of value for each asset that cannot be altered without changing the underlying asset value. The proof/stake methodology also directly addresses the concerns of users who are concerned that their assets could be subject to abuse.

In the distributed system of solar, each node acts as a vote. When a user verifies that an asset has a specific value, he receives a vote that validates his claim. Each round of voting adds more nodes into the solar cluster until eventually, the network distributes into hundreds or thousands of individual ledgers.

Because the distribution of the ledger is decentralized, there is no centralization risk. Unlike traditional blockchains where some nodes hold the majority of the balance, Solana uses a quorum system, which means that a set number of nodes must be present for a ledger to operate. The combination of a strong proof-of-stake mechanism and the number of users allowed in the network to ensure that the nodes remain coherent and do not collude to take advantage of the honest users of the network's power.

Since the Solana protocol is based on proof of work (POW), it prevents the possibility of an attacker controlling the network and making unlimited funds transfers. If he were to do so, he could easily double-spend existing assets. Because every transaction in the solar network is a new transaction, each of them is timestamped and stored in the blockchain. Each time you commit to doing business with a user, you are also making a transaction in the blockchain along with him, proving that you have both agreed upon the terms of the transaction and are both aware of what it entails.

Chapter 23 – Solana: The New Cryptocompetition

Solana is a new digital currency that intends to replace all traditional money as well as paper checks with its own highly secure and efficient digital currency. Unlike other digital currencies, it has no prerequisites to maintain. It is entirely dependent on its user community to keep it running smoothly. The currency is not centralized in any way and exists to cater to the needs of each community.

Solana utilizes smart contracts to host decentralized apps (apps). But Solana on different parameters for its operation allows it to offer much cheaper transaction fees while simultaneously increasing the rate of the network. The developers chose a Proof-of-Concept (PoC) approach wherein the system combines three popular components - the IaaS, iControl, and the Transaction Scalar Networks. The combination creates what cryptographers refer to as the "safe" environment where security is ensured without compromising the overall system security. The result is that users can conduct instant and one-click secure transactions.

Unlike other digital currencies, such as Dash and Zcash, which have had problems adjusting to slow transaction speeds due to the network's block times, Solana uses a proof-of-work (POW) system to generate block times that are guaranteed. The proof-of-work approach was chosen because it increases the likelihood that a new node will be added to the network resulting in fast and secure transactions. Since most PoCs available at launch time had poor PoW performance, their assumption that faster block times will bring in more users proves faulty. In addition, this system allows for true decentralized scalability.

However, the biggest problem faced by businesses looking to use the ethereum as their fundraising mechanism lies in its dependency on centralized exchanges. While a decentralized network like the one proposed by the creators would ensure fair distribution of stakers, distributors, and lenders, centralized exchanges make the system highly dependent on a few large players. If one of them goes bankrupt, the other ones cannot function. This poses a serious threat to the future development of the decentralized altcoin community.

The creators of Solana have addressed this problem by building a decentralized validator mechanism. Unlike a regular validator, the decentralized validator system involves a process that ensures only the holders of a certain transaction happen to be listed on the validated list. In other words, every time someone requests a validation, his request is sent to all other validators and the list of participants is modified accordingly. Once all the participants are listed, only then will the list be validated and the request is approved. While this system may sound complex, it greatly reduces the possibility of one particular group manipulating the list, thereby breaking the distribution chain and possibly damaging the entire ecosystem of the cryptocoin ecosystem.

Apart from this added layer of security, the creators of Solana have also designed a robust staking plan to ensure that tokens obtained through the staking plan are only diverted towards the correct project. They include parameters for determining the number of tokens to be distributed as well as the manner in which the tokens will be allocated. Through the use of tokens, those who participate will be able to convert their assets into actual currency, thus maximizing their potential returns.

Chapter 24 - What Is Uniswap and How Does It Work?

Uniswap, a decentralized alternative to the traditional exchange, is an ever-evolving protocol that enables anyone to trade any digital asset using a smart contract. It offers several benefits over other traditional forex trading systems: it allows you to trade using a virtual online trading account; you can trade almost any altcoin or cryptocurrency pair at any time; you can customize your risk/reward profile; and best of all, you can do all this without a broker! Furthermore, unlike other systems, you don't need to download any software or maintain any websites.

The original Uniswap was released in November 2018 and continues to add new features to the protocol. These include higher leverage levels, faster transaction processing times, and higher liquidity. In 2021, the Uniswap V3 has recently been released, adding several new features as well as we discuss in this chapter.

One of the most important features of the Uniswap decentralized exchanges is their increased liquidity. Because it does not use a broker, you have instant access to real-time quotes on all major altcoins. Because it is decentralized, you don't have to worry about paying high transaction fees to third parties - you'll be able to cut these costs by conducting most of your business transactions yourself. Because the liquidity is higher, you will have more opportunities to trade, thus increasing your profits. This feature has been instrumental in improving the performance of the Uniswap.

Another feature of the Uniswap protocol is the Hayden Adams automated program. This automated trading system is designed to react to changes in the market and generate profitable trades for traders. Since the automated system is based on real-time quotes from Uniswap, this allows traders to reduce their risk of holding currencies that may not have increased in value. In addition, since the automated system is based on non-upgradeable smart contracts on the Ethereum blockchain, it improves the accuracy and validity of the Uniswap market.

When you visit the official Uniswap website, you'll see the interface which is available to give direction to the decentralized exchange by updating the price of the traded swap tokens between the two currencies.

The underlying technology behind Uniswap is an open-source decentralized platform. This is what makes the trades happen in the system. Traders can choose to open a new trade by clicking on the "New Trade" button that takes them to a screen where they can specify the asset they wish to trade (the currency pair of the chosen Uniswap currency pair). Next, they click on "Trade". Finally, they enter a sell and buy to place their order with the broker.

The tokens to be exchanged in the uniswap are ERC-20 tokens that are based on the real-time transaction price of ether from the Ethereum network. The ERC-20 tokens used for Uniswap trades are transferable and are not limited in supply.

Chapter 25 – Uniswap: A Hybrid Investment Platform

Uniswap, which was developed by members of the Open Ledger Project (OLP), is an innovative approach to transfer funds in the world of Cryptocurrency. Uniswap functions through an entirely decentralized network of brokers, rather than the traditional exchange of funds between traders and investors. Instead of being limited to trade only through exchanges and brokerages, Uniswap enables any user to conduct all financial business on the same network. Through this approach, any individual or company can operate in the volatile world of Cryptocurrency. This chapter will provide some more insight into the Uniswap project and how it differs from other leading Cryptocurrency protocols.

One of the biggest advantages of Uniswap over other leading protocols is its design as a token-issuing protocol. Uniswap works through a token system, rather than a conventional exchange of currency. As such, users can easily exchange any token without the need for conventional exchanges. The token system is used as the digital currency unit of account. Through this innovative approach, users can monitor and manage their finances on a decentralized network, as opposed to a traditional system where one organization controls the trading volume and can dictate how funds are invested.

Through the launch of the Uniswap software, the network of brokers who supported the protocol's development was able to offer greater functionality for their clients. In addition, several new features were added to the Uniswap software as well, to further enhance its utility and performance for users. Some of these features include the ability to manage multiple token wallets, the ability to monitor and manage your funds daily, and the ability to transact on the Ethereum network. Today, the protocol is available in a v3 upgrade, which adds the following new features.

One of the most interesting features of Uniswap that makes it distinct from other top-down crypto networks is its highly efficient distribution method. Distributed ledger technology offers several benefits for any program in terms of scalability, efficiency, and reliability. With that said, a traditional ledger used to track the funds available in a traditional blockchain environment would require a massive bandwidth and massive storage space to function. With Uniswap, a new approach was taken to handling the distributed ledger. Instead of having each ledger on its block or series of blocks, the entire process is done on a proof-of-stake basis. As such, each investor will only be able to create an account with a certain value of their choosing as collateral.

An additional feature of Uniswap that sets it apart from other top-down Cryptocurrency network programs is its use of a hybrid smart-contract system called the ERC-20 protocol. Traders and investors can execute risk management and transaction funding through a digital asset, known as tokens. The use of these tokens instead of real money allows investors to avoid the possibility of fines and restrictions.

Another unique feature of Uniswap that distinguishes it from other top-down Cryptocurrency programs is its integration of social trading. Unlike some top-down Cryptocurrencies that only allow traders to execute transactions within their network, users can now interact with each other and form their networks within the same platform. This has the potential to greatly increase the liquidity of tokens and therefore, increase the demand for them. In fact, following the announcement of Uniswap launch, many new names have come out in the Cryptocurrency trading space, all vying for the rights to profit from the Uniswap program.

The biggest appeal of Uniswap however, is its use of tokens as the source of value. By creating an open-source platform that allows its users to swap the tokens they hold, Uniswap ensures that it provides true liquidity by eliminating the problems associated with centralized exchanges. While traditional exchanges look to impose large trading fees onto traders, Uniswap eliminates these fees through its zero trading fee policy. In addition to eliminating fees, users of Uniswap can also enjoy a more passive form of income.

Finally, users of the Uniswap platform will benefit from the increased level of security that comes with being part of a decentralized exchange. Through the use of its token-based financing mechanism, users are provided with a flexible, cost-effective method of securing capital. By decentralizing trade in this manner, Uniswap gives itself the ability to respond faster and more effectively to market changes and improve liquidity. By combining a token-based financing system with increased liquidity and security, Uniswap has created one of the most unique hybrid private equity investment models.

Chapter 26 - Learning More About the Bitcoin Cash (BCH)

Figure: Note the sign says Bitcoin (not Bitcoin Cash). Many novices mix these up. Bitcoin Cash (BCH) might be promising, but it is not the original Bitcoin (BTC). So don't mistake an altcoin (BCH) for King Bitcoin (BTC).

Cryptocurrency is money that is stored, traded, and generally handled electronically through networks. The most popular example of this is called Bitcoin. With the use of various techniques and strategies, people can easily convert one currency to another or spend their funds from one currency to another without having to wait for conventional payment methods to change hands. There are two main elements to Cryptocurrency: Digital Asset and Financial Asset.

The developers of Bitcoin Cash decided to fork the original Bitcoin due to several reasons. Most notably was the perception that there were not sufficient fees being paid to users who had migrated to the new fork. The developers felt that this was a reflection of the lack of true value of bitcoin cash itself. This gave rise to BIP 11, the code that will change the way that fees are paid. Once this was released, the network behind Bitcoin Cash began to split into two factions.

Miners are those who secure the network and decide how much they want to invest in the system by producing additional blocks of digital assets that are included in each transaction. The new block system called BIP 13 decides how these miners are designated and what they must pay to be included in the network. Groups that have interests in this include the Core Developers, Software Developers, and Full-Service Providers.

The Core Developers are developers who write most of the code that makes up the backbone of the system. They are also the individuals who decide which modifications are made to the code and how they are compatible with the rest of the community. The purpose of the Core Developers is to maintain the safety and value of the decentralized ledger that is used as the backbone of the entire bitcoin cash system. If something major is to go wrong with the system then the Core Developers will be the ones who will deal with the issue. Their job is to make sure that all users are protected from any problems that may come about as a result of the modifications being made to the protocol.

Another group with interest in Bitcoin Cash is the individuals who develop software tools that are needed to implement the features of the bitcoin cash system. These tools will then be submitted to the miners for them to use in their mining operations. The main objective of the software developers group is to help the miners make more money, which is the overall purpose of their job. With the software tools, miners can easily increase the amount of money that they mine and they can also decrease the amount of money that they spend in the process. They are there to serve as middlemen between users and the decentralized ledger that make up the entire system.

The Full-Service Provider group, as the name suggests, are the companies that will handle all of the services necessary for the deployment of the new blocks of the cryptocurrency. They include the building and maintaining of the mining equipment as well as ensuring that the client software applications are compatible with the new blocks. When it comes to security, these entities must stay completely up to date on the newest developments as this can greatly impact their ability to protect the network. In addition, these entities are also responsible for creating the new blocks as well as supervising their workers.

One of the most exciting aspects of the bitcoin cash system is the fact that it is now possible for individuals to conduct full activities within the system without having to rely on a third party. This is made possible by the way that the system can handle transactions between multiple parties that have an account with the digital currency. As you may have guessed, the technology was born from the community known as the bitcoin cash. This group of people wanted to create a way for everyday consumers to spend their money using a new form of electronic cash.

It is important to understand that the use of this type of technology is not intended to replace the current system that works in the real world. The developers of this alternate form of currency want to foster more economic freedom for all who use the bitcoin protocol. It is their goal to create a situation where people can spend their money without having to go through unnecessary hassles and stay out of debt.

Chapter 27 – BCH: a stable and secure Bitcoin fork

If you are interested in learning more about altcoins such as Bitcoin Cash, then you will want to read this chapter. Specifically, we'll discuss some history of the altcoin, how it began trading on various currency exchanges, its future potential as a lucrative investment vehicle, and whether or not it has proved to be a successful alternative to the traditional methods used to trade the crypto market.

First of all, let's take a look at the background of bitcoin cash. It was developed by two companies working together to create an alternative to the mainstream currencies being traded on online exchanges. Their idea was to have faster transaction times along with lower costs associated with the on-chain transfer of data. They wanted to "simplify" the way people make trades on the chain.

When they created the new technology known as SegWit, it solved two problems that had been occurring with the previous alternatives. The first problem was scalability. With scalability, smaller blocks could be created to accommodate higher volumes of transfers. This was necessary so that the average size of a block could be increased without negatively affecting performance.

With the creation of SegWit, the second problem was increased block size. The average transaction size is around 2.5 MB and as more users adopt this new protocol, scalability will become an issue. The solution is the implementation of a larger block alongside the SegWit technology. By doing this, more transactions per second can be handled while still maintaining good scalability.

However, if you're unfamiliar with the details of how the hard fork was developed, you may not understand why scalability is such an issue for the new cryptocurrency. When two forks are created, one must remain stable and secure while the other is rejected and consequently replaced. The Bitcoin Cash project was no different; however, they needed to prevent the long-term damage that a single negative fork could cause.

The entire industry is taking advantage of the opportunity that the hard fork offers. To take advantage of the rise in the value of alternate currencies, you need to be aware of what's happening in the world of bitcoin cash and altcoins.

You must keep up on the latest news about the different blockchains. You need to know how the protocol and the ecosystem will react to any changes, so you don't get caught off guard and trade against the flow. The future of crypto coinage remains uncertain, but there's no doubt that investors are excited by the potential of the technology. This future, however, is still far off and the recent hard work is just one step closer to changing the landscape of the future.

With regard to what's next for the future of bitcoins and altcoin communities, it's safe to say that the future for the crypto coinage looks bright but is far from clear. However, the bright future that most investors are anticipating is good news for anyone that has been waiting for a safe return on their investment in the currency.

Chapter 28 – Litecoin is Still One of the Fastest Growing Altcoins

Litecoin (LTC) is an innovative peer-to-peer Cryptocurrency and open source software project developed under an open-source license. Litecoin was an early spin-off of parallel currency, Bitcoin, beginning in 2011. In simple technical terms, Litecoin differs from other cryptocurrencies in that it uses an altered proof of work system (aka proof of stake) than most coins. Proof of work involves having a certain amount of Litecoin awarded to each individual that will participate in the network. This award is referred to as stake or cap in many instances.

By 2021, Litecoin had become one of the fastest-growing virtual currencies in the world. This was largely due to the fact that Litecoin has no fundamental problems with supply or demand. In the decade since its launch, it went from being worth less than a dollar to over one hundred dollars.

The surge in popularity of Litecoin resulted in an increase in its supply, which peaked at over twenty-five percent. This was primarily due to Litecoin developers releasing the Litecoin Testnet. Litecoin Testnet is a closed source program that allows users to test the functionality of various aspects of the Litecoin protocol. Users may test Litecoin on their personal computers and connect to the testnet network via an Internet connection. Once accepted into the main Litecoin community, the Testnet would provide a gateway for individuals to start using the main Litecoin client without the need to take a risk with real money.

The popularity of Litecoin ultimately led to its inclusion in the main Litecoin ledger, called the blockchain. Once on the chain, Litecoin could be traded as an ordinary cryptocurrency by individuals all over the world. The use of the decentralized infrastructure called the blockchain would allow for instant global trades, a feature currently missing in the centralized blockchain.

One of the unique features of Litecoin that makes it different from other cryptocurrencies is its recognition of the lesser a transaction is made, the more money the market maker is able to capture. Litecoin's unique incentive system also enables it to implement a "mining" mechanism. With a "mining" function, Litecoin miners are rewarded based on the difficulty of generating new blocks. More miners joining the pool will result in an increased difficulty and thus the ability to mint newer units of Litecoin.

At its inception, Litecoin had a circulating supply of approximately twenty-four million coins. As of late 2021, this has expanded to sixty-seven million coins. The exact number of circulating litecoins is subject to change depending on the demand on the market. However, this figure does not account for the number of individuals that hold unconfirmed Litecoins. The total supply of Litecoin is capped at 84 million LTC, analogous to Bitcoin's capped supply of 21 million BTC. Therefore, like Bitcoin and many of the altcoins discussed in this book, Litecoin, is also deflationary since its supply is capped. (By contrast, stablecoins like USDT, are not deflationary because they are linked to fiat currency. So stablecoin supply must increase every time governments print more fiat currency.)

At the time of publication of this book, Litecoin has been attributed with a market capitalization of nearly 12 billion US dollars.

Chapter 29 - Litecoin: The Original Crypto 'Silver'

Litecoin (LTC) is an open-source and peer-to-peer virtual currency and digital asset. Litecoin was an early experimental spin-off of Bitcoin, beginning in October 2011. It was often called 'silver' in the early days of cryptocurrencies when Bitcoin was often considered analogous to 'gold'. However, today, Litecoin itself has a few competitors for the number 2 (silver) spot on the coin market cap index. Nonetheless, Litecoin has proved its value over time and continues to be a competitive altcoin.

Exchanges and sales of litecoin are done directly between users on the network. Because of this feature, Litecoin can be thought of as an alternative to "virtual money" such as the majority of prepaid credit cards and online shopping cart systems.

One major difference between Litecoin and other currencies is that it does not handle any liabilities like the majority of the world's currencies do. This is good news for new investors, who do not want to hold large amounts of unmonetized assets, and is especially appealing to investors who need to have their monies in one location and are not concerned about how those assets will be valued in the future. Since Litecoin transactions cannot be tied back to any particular currency, no central bank needs to be involved, and like many other altcoins, no regulatory guidelines govern the process. This is another attraction for new investors who may not be comfortable with the idea of investing their money in centrally controlled countries where the process of money transfer can be complex and slow.

Another benefit of Litecoin is that it can be traded anonymously through what is called a mixer network. This is done through a specialized software program that registers individual Litecoin addresses and then mixes the coins that are being traded. An investor who sends an order to enter the market must have a private key that can be used to sign onto the Litecoin mixer server and enter the market. Once there, he will receive his funds, and that the transaction will be recorded on the Litecoin ledger. This system prevents direct interaction between individual investors, which makes Litecoin an attractive option for private investors.

One advantage of Litecoin is that it takes only 2.5 min to complete a transaction. This is because it has a shorter hops algorithm and because it works with a slightly faster network than the main Bitcoin network. It is worth pointing out that this is much less than the 8 to 10-minute average transaction time that the main Bitcoin network requires.

As one of the original contenders, Litecoin has maintained a close race with Bitcoin for a decade. In the future, we may see an influx of new altcoins built off the Litecoin open-source code, which in turn is an original Bitcoin derivative. For now, though, we will just have to wait and see what happened with the previous cryptocurrencies that tried to emulate Litecoins but gradually faded away. There will also be other altcoins built on other networks that will continue to try and displace both the originals: Litecoin 'silver' and King Bitcoin 'gold'.

Chapter 30 – Chainlink for Hybrid Smart Contracts

Chainlink (LINK) is an Ethereum-based virtual token that serves as a backend connection to internal data sources, internal APIs, and payment mechanisms. This network enables smart contracts on the ethereum network to safely connect to external third-party data sources, external APIs, and internal payment systems without exposing any sensitive information to these third parties. The aim of this network is to create a real-time secured connection between two or more interacting smart contract programs through an encrypted channel. As a result, smart contract programmers have unfettered access to multiple types of data, resources, and channels, which are critical in building highly interactive online business models and applications.

As with any other token decentralized oracle network, users participate in the Chainlink process by requesting nodes to join the network at specific intervals. These nodes are called "chainlinks", and there are currently 5 billion total chain links. Each time one of these links is completed, the other nodes join the queue, and so the whole system becomes a self-sustaining, self-guarding, Byzantine Fault Tolerance (BFT) network. If any malicious nodes manage to get on the network, this Byzantine Fault Tolerance system will kick into action and all transactions will be halted until the attackers are taken out of the queue.

The token used in the system, Chainlink, is mined from the Ethereum network. By using an algorithm that ensures that the same people will participate in creating a new Chainlink, the distribution of tokens is controlled roughly equally. There is no centralization or "central" control of Chainlink. Just like the other currencies in the system, there is an unlimited supply, meaning that new tokens can be easily and cheaply created. With a limited supply, the supply is only constricted by the amount that certain individuals or businesses decide to contribute to the distribution of tokens.

The way that the entire work is simple - nodes that participate in the Byzantine Fault Tolerance process buy or sell back tokens from others in the system. Once each transaction has been completed, the seller of the token receives a certain fixed percentage of the sale, plus whatever fees were involved. In the long run, it is theoretically possible for someone to reach a distribution point of nearly one trillion tokens, which would make an ICO token worth thousands of US dollars each. This, of course, depends on whether or not the government decides to add a regulating body to the Cryptocurrency Act.

Many people who have decided to participate in the ICO craze are avid traders who hope that the rise in market cap will help them realize their financial independence. Others are speculators who see the trend as nothing more than a bubble that will burst soon enough. The latter group seems to view the rising value of currencies as a chance to profit off of the "tulip" effect. For every two hundred thousand Tulips being sold, one speculator could receive five.

In the meantime, investors who have joined in on the chainlink bandwagon are finding that they can trade anonymously with ease. It is entirely possible to set up an account that will allow you to gamble on altcoins that you purchase from the main pool. While this isn't ideal for those who wish to use a stable currency to participate in the ICO hype, it does offer some anonymity.

Chainlink does have its disadvantages for beginners, however.

The two drawbacks that most people think of when they consider investing in either Cryptocurrencies or Altcoins like Chainlink are the difficulty of learning how to set up wallets and how to access their private keys. With the recent news about the leaking of a huge cache of confidential information belonging to Chainlink traders, the need to learn how to manage your private key has become even more crucial. As long as you keep your private key safe then you will have no problem transitioning into the new altcoin marketplace. The other important consideration with investing in both Cryptocurrencies and Altcoins is how well the protocol is designed. Some altcoins such as Chainlink are newer than many others, but the protocol that is being used on it is not only different but also much more advanced than any other altcoin in the same category. There is always room for innovation in any area, and it is safe to say that altcoins like Chainlink will continue to expand as the technology behind them matures.

Chapter 31 - Using Chainlink For Your Cryptocurrency Project

Chainlink (LINK) is an Ethereum-based virtual currency that enables the Chainlink digital public ledger. This public ledger is a replicated interactive database where all transactions are logged and recorded in a secure manner. Transactions are executed within the same chain, ensuring instant confirmation and execution. The system uses smart contracts to facilitate money transfers and other business applications. This system allows for secure, scalable, permission-protected, and distributed collaboration.

Chainlink significantly expands the capabilities of smart contracts by providing access to real-world data and off-chain computing, while maintaining the reliability and security which is a key feature of blockchain technology.

The main focus of the Chainlink developers was to build a better system for digital agreements, especially smart contract platforms that run along with public networks. The team succeeded in designing and building several hundred smart oracles based on several open-source projects. Several hundred smart oracles are already running in production and are being deployed in various environments across the world.

The Chainlink system is comprised of two major components - Chainlink tokens or sets of ether and other digital currencies, and the Chainlink application oracles. The tokens or ether forms the base of the system, while the other two components, such as the application oracles, provide additional functionality. The tokens can be used to purchase services from external companies. These services are then indirectly reflected in the value of the ether. The Chainlink smart contracts ensure instant execution of the transactions.

There are several types of the Chainlink smart contract. The original Chainlink system consists of two types of nodes. The first set of nodes are known as the "parent" nodes. These nodes are responsible for spreading the information among all the other connected nodes. The second type of node is referred to as the "child" node.

The developers have planned several improvements to the original Chainlink protocol. For instance, they have introduced a new type of smart contract that provides an improved level of privacy. The new feature uses dummy nodes to send the transactions without broadcasting them to the network. This improved form of the Chainlink is called the "blockchain oracle" technology.

However, during the past years, the developers have successfully combined the ideas of the original Chainlink with the latest innovations in the market.

Next, let's discuss each of the Chainlink elements. First, the tokens are used to represent the Off-Chain sources and the smart contract is used to transfer the tokens from the On-Chain sources to the buyers. And also, let's discuss the usage of the Chainlink data provided by the smart contract.

It's important to note the working process of the off-chain and on-chain networks. However, one thing must be noted that no matter what technology is being used in the smart contract, users still need to adhere to the fundamental rules of the chainlink. Therefore, it is important to avoid performing any unnecessary transactions or linking chains without sufficient backup information. Although there are several advantages of the off-chain systems, including its privacy and control features, users must be careful enough to avoid abuse of the system.

The token buyers and sellers can perform many functions like transferring funds, accessing other smart contracts, accessing the underlying real-time data feeds, and recording the addresses of other participants in the transaction. Besides, the Chainlink is not susceptible to denial of service attacks since all messages are broadcasted over the wide-area network. The token buyers are protected from such attacks by using a decentralized oracle network, which is an internet that consists of several different IP networks. By utilizing such a decentralized oracle system, the users are protected from any attacks, either during the execution of the smart contract or afterward.

Smart contract buyers and sellers need to ensure that they are not agreeing to any kind of double-spending. Furthermore, users of this technology should make sure that they do not start their Chainlink project before they have adequate research and development in place. This way, once their projects start taking off, they can easily attain profits without having to resort to any tricks.

If you want to participate in the exciting world of tokens and smart contracts, then consider looking into Chainlink. Unlike other currencies and commodities, the token and its trading prices are based entirely on the performance of the projects it represents. Therefore, by participating in these projects you can instantly gain profit while helping the industry grow. In addition to this, there is no physical cash or currency involved, so the risks are significantly reduced. This makes Chainlink an attractive option for anyone interested in building a business in the digital economy.

PART 4 – HOW TO INVEST IN AND STORE ALTCOINS

In this section, we'll introduce you to some cryptocurrency exchanges where you can purchase cryptocurrencies such as bitcoins and emerging altcoins discussed in this book. We'll also discuss some of the best options for storing them for safekeeping.

Chapter 32 - What Popular Cryptocurrency Exchanges Have in Common

Cryptocurrency exchanges are online companies that allow clients to trade traditional fiat currency or virtual currencies for cryptocurrencies or other virtual currencies. Their popularity has increased in recent times as the value of the crypto market has grown. Many large financial institutions and other leading businesses have also entered into this field.

As far as how these services operate, here is some information. A typical marketplace includes several monetary units that are either held by users themselves, held by the marketplace itself, or are traded between users on the behalf of users. The process for transferring between these currencies is usually done through a software platform that has been built specifically for that purpose. Various types of currencies can be traded on these exchanges including Bitcoin, Ethereum, and the Altcoins discussed in this book. These are just some of the more popular and more stable currencies being traded on the Crypto exchanges.

These platforms offer several advantages over the traditional over-the-counter market. First of all, they offer increased liquidity, meaning that more buyers and sellers can potentially influence the market. This increased liquidity means that we traders can make more accurate predictions about movements within the market and as a result, can take advantage of opportunities to make more money.

The best way to select the best platform to use is to analyze what your needs are. For example, if you like to trade larger, high-quality coins then you may want to use a reputable and well-established platform. Also, if you like to have the freedom to enter and exit the market at any time and have a fast turnaround time, then consider the liquidity that your broker offers as an important factor. Finally, if you are unfamiliar with the crypto exchange that is being traded you may want to request access to a demo platform until you are familiar with the platform and ready to trade with real money.

The advantage of a demo account at a crypto exchange is that it allows you to place fictitious trades without risking any real money. Some demo platforms look very realistic, so always double-check that it is in fact demo and not a real account until you have obtained sufficient practice. For your real account, if you are trading large or interest-bearing coins you will likely need to be familiar with some basic understanding of cryptocurrencies such as that presented in this book. As you gain experience as a cryptocurrency trader, you will become familiar with the market and the altcoins of interest to you the more you practice.

Trading cryptocurrencies could be a topic of a whole new book, and it is a rather advanced topic. For this reason, this current book focuses mostly on investing, rather than trading. And the emphasis is placed on higher quality altcoins that can have significant value as investments.

In the coming months and years, there will be many more regulatory changes that will impact the marketplace. Many of these changes will be implemented in the United States and some in the United Kingdom. There are also other regulatory changes anticipated around the world. Cryptocurrency exchange trading platforms should be prepared for any regulatory changes that may be implemented so that they can properly meet the needs of their customers. If they do not adapt their services to meet the regulatory changes and continue to allow access to the marketplace to the unscrupulous elements of the digital currency exchange business, it will be difficult for those people and businesses to continue to operate.

One of the features that Cryptocurrency Exchanges look for in potential members is a commitment to maintaining safety and privacy at all times. Both customers and service providers want their information to remain private and safe from outside influences. This is one of the major reasons why investors in the Cryptocurrency exchange business are willing to spend a sizeable amount of money on these types of services. In the future, more regulatory agencies will look closely at how Cryptocurrency use protects their users and will likely require additional protections.

Another feature that certain Cryptocurrency Exchanges look for in potential members is a good understanding of their trading volumes. Exchanges need reliable liquidity if they are to offer competitive prices to both buyers and sellers. They cannot rely on their members having large and liquid inventories. Liquidity means a business has adequate levels of supply and demand of the virtual currency it is trading and there are reliable and liquid liquidity providers available in the marketplace.

The final Cryptocurrency Exchange feature that many traders look for in a prospective member is a good and secure user interface for the platform itself. A user-friendly and efficient dashboard is necessary to ensure the most efficient operation of the Cryptocurrency Exchange and that the process of buying and selling can be done with minimal risk. All information about the various assets being traded should be displayed and easy to access and navigate. All transactions should be processed quickly and easily and the entire marketplace should be liquid enough for any new investor or trader to get into the market and start building their portfolio. Most importantly, though, the Cryptocurrency Exchange needs to have good security and a reputation for fair play.

Chapter 33 - Compare the Best Cryptocurrency Exchanges For Your Trading Needs

In an economic system with multiple players, the value of each player's currency changes based on the value of the others. The value of a single currency usually cannot be measured in absolute terms, because it depends on the wishes of each participant in the economic system. The best Cryptocurrency Exchanges provide the most comprehensive and convenient way for traders to participate in the global market.

To choose the best Cryptocurrency exchanges, it is advisable to research each one. This is best done by looking at how they interact with the market. Some of the best ones are Coinbase.com, Binance.us (US), and Binance.com (International). Each one has a different method of operation, and each one is unique when it comes to the number of trades that take place each day. Although most offer a large variety of coins, each crypto exchange is subject to local regulations and the altcoins that each exchange can offer do vary.

However, for the most part, the prominent cryptocoins discussed in this book are available in most cryptocurrency exchanges. The best investors and traders ensure that trades are executed through brokers who have the appropriate experience in the industry.

The best Cryptocurrency exchanges should also have excellent customer service and security features. These should be available at all times, twenty-four hours a day. This is important, especially if you are using your trading platform to trade in other currencies as well as coins with virtual currencies. It is important to ensure that you are protected from hackers who may try to use your personal information to extract funds from you. The best companies will always protect their clients' information and ensure that they are responsibly conducting business.

The best Cryptocurrency exchanges will also regulate the trading activity of their customers. They will do this to ensure that there is fair trading and that the rules and regulations governing the use of their currencies are complied with. Regulation of exchanges is necessary in order to protect both the investors and the asset owners. This helps to maintain the integrity and efficiency of the marketplace and ensures that the supply of bitcoins and altcoins can keep up with the demand created by investors. Investors and traders will be able to buy and sell crypto coins with real cash value, allowing them to continue investing in their chosen asset class, and are earning money along the way. Note that regulation has both pros and cons, but when used wisely by a reputable broker, it can be beneficial for traders. For most investors, after your purchase, it may be wisest to move your cryptocoins off the exchanges to your personal e-wallet. Most good e-wallets that store cryptocurrencies offline especially cannot be regulated. So if you decide to take complete control of your cryptocurrencies with an offline wallet, just don't lose your private keys.

When searching for the best Cryptocurrency exchanges, it is important to find one that has a good reputation that will not only be based on your experience but will also be based on the experience of others. Do not invest in any company that does not have an excellent reputation or does not offer reliable online platforms. However, even with a reputable crypto exchange, losses are possible if you decide to become a trader without much experience. Keep in mind that many beginners will make mistakes when trading and can lose large amounts of money due to inexperience. Investing (rather than trading) in good cryptocurrencies for the long term may be a better strategy for most beginners.

When comparing various Cryptocurrency exchanges, consider the best features each offer. Look at which company offers the best tools for you to learn about the world of trading, including tools that allow you to watch the market and keep track of your portfolio. Do not invest in a company that does not offer an excellent trading platform, as you will likely need this in order to get started. In addition to a great website and education program, the best Cryptocurrency exchanges will provide excellent customer service. Some of the best companies offer 24-hour customer support so you can be sure to receive answers to all of your questions.

Finding out more information about these top-rated crypto exchanges and their trading options should not be difficult, as their websites are very accessible. Take some time to review the information they provide on their websites and familiarize yourself with how the market may affect them. We will continue this discussion of crypto exchanges in more depth in the subsequent chapters.

Chapter 34 - Binance - A New Trading Way For the Cryptocurrency Market

Binance is well-known for its fast trade execution. Before company founder Changpeng Zhao began Binance in China in late 2017, he designed a software platform for matching orders for fast-moving traders. Binance has courted controversy with regulators, proceeding with operations out of China to Japan; later in a May 2018 keynote address, Zhao said that the parent firm does not have a physical location because only virtual currencies do have an office. The company has also expanded to other markets including the United States. If you're thinking about investing in the crypto-financial market, Binance may be a good choice for you.

Binance also offers a variety of investing methods, including options trading, venture investment funds, and several cryptocoins in addition to options. Cryptocurrency trading is growing in popularity across many different sectors of the global economy. Trading in this sector has increased around double-digit percentages over the last year, reaching new highs each year. As this trend continues, more people will be able to participate in this popular investment opportunity on international crypto exchanges like Binance.

To participate in the Binance exchange, you will need to have funds in your Binance account before trading can commence. There are no minimum amounts of funds, and you can start trading as low as five hundred dollars per trade. One of the most attractive features of Binance is that it offers free account management. This includes daily trades that are managed by professional traders. If you are unfamiliar with this type of account management, Binance offers a free Binance demo account where you can practice different strategies and see what the impact on your portfolio will be. You can use this same information to help guide you in the growth of your Binance investment.

Many people are investing in Binance because it offers a cost-effective way to trade using alternate currencies. If you look around, you can find that trading commodities and other goods with alternative currencies can be very profitable. However, there is only so much that you can do without relying on traditional methods of banking. Those methods include paying brokers who have access to information on all exchanges, checking bank statements, and waiting for the government to make announcements about which currencies should be legal tender. With the introduction of Binance, people can trade with any currency that they want. This makes it much easier to participate in the Binance exchange since you do not need to change your methods of trading.

Even if you are not an experienced trader, you can still benefit from the Binance exchange. Because it uses one of the most well-known and reliable marketplaces, Binance is very accessible. Anyone interested in trading can get into the game relatively quickly. Once you set up an account with Binance, you can start with a mini test drive using one of their funded test accounts. This allows you to build your confidence and learn the ins and outs of the Binance marketplace before going live.

With your Binance test fund, you can develop your strategies for trading. This helps you get a feel for the market without having to pay fees for using the Binance marketplace. Binance does offer a currency pairing demo that lets you put in trades with virtual money to see how it feels like to be trading in real-time with real money. The Binance team has done a great job designing an online trading platform that is accessible from anywhere. You can even use your smartphone or tablet to execute your trades on the Binance dashboard.

Binance is currently ranked in the top three major crypto exchanges. If you are looking to get into the game quickly and easily, it is highly recommended that you look into Binance. Binance also provides users with several instructional videos that walk you through the steps involved in the trading process. By following these steps, you should have no problem getting into the game and becoming profitable soon.

Chapter 35 – Binance Can Exchange Dollars For Your Favorite Altcoins

Almost every jurisdiction in the globe has its regulations on what is or what is not allowed in their location. So for traders and cryptocurrency investors, your acceptance by a specific broker could depend solely on your geographical location. Binance currently has branches in a few local markets, including Binance US. For international investors, Binance.com is the most popular. Binance.com was the original version of Binance and is still available to international investors. However, to comply with US laws, Binance.US was also established for US residents.

Although the selection of tokens is slightly less at Binance US, it still has the largest marketplace of tokens compared to any other virtual currency exchange available for US residents.

Binance charges a base rate plus commission for each trade. However, this rate changes constantly based on current market conditions. They have an average rate across the board, but the rate varies significantly between pairs due to differences in overall supply and demand, among other factors. This means traders can get a large rate breakthrough spread betting or by shorting certain pairs due to the higher liquidity factor involved.

Even though Binance has relatively high trading, it has the most flexible and least expensive platform. Their main page has an extensive list of cryptocurrencies and their rates against each other, but you can search for a currency pair of your choice and find out its cost against each other. You also have the option to search for a list of all historical prices to compare cryptocurrencies against each other. This makes it easy for beginners to find profitable pairs to invest in. Binance also offers several instructional videos and resources for new users.

Both Binance.com and Binance.us have an abundance of features including simple conversions, advanced trading, and margin trading. Binance.com also offers derivatives, leverage token trading, and even options trading of cryptocurrencies. After signing up, it's a good idea to spend some time on their website, reading the info, and watching their videos, before investing a significant amount in their exchanges. For long-term cryptocurrency investors, you may just want to use Binance as a way to convert your dollars into your favorite altcoins. If that's the case, you can just stick to the simple 'convert' feature which they offer. After the conversion of your dollars to your new altcoin, you can then move your altcoin off the exchange to your favorite e-wallet or hardware wallet for long-term storage.

Chapter 36 - Using Coinbase to Trade or Invest in Cryptocurrencies

Coinbase is a good place to start if you want to learn more about the latest developments in the world of digital currencies. The website allows anyone to register with them free of charge. This will allow them to take advantage of the platform's "wallets" function, which lets them store their coins in an account with funds that are automatically withdrawn when they are spent. Coinbase has been created by two notable venture capitalists, Brian Armstrong and Fred Ehrsam.

Coinbase is a well-known cryptocurrency exchange, serving both institutional investors and everyday consumers. In April 2021, Coinbase became a publically listed company on Nasdaq with stock ticker symbol COIN. The platform offers over 50 pre-composed cryptocurrency assets, bitcoin, ethereum, Cardano, and many more altcoins. To get started, you will need at least $100 to open up your account, but be ready to scour through different fees. Fees could increase once the platform begins additional uncommon altcoins cryptocurrency assets.

There are two methods of payment on Coinbase. You can either pay with a credit card or via a major credit card or debit card. If you intend to make deposits or make purchases using your Cryptocurrency investments, you must pay the flat fee. The flat fee charged to you is only a one-time transaction fee, which is taken for all transactions, not just deposits or purchases. The average consumer will not see any difference in their bottom line by making the flat fee payment.

Coinbase allows its users to create a customized trading platform. The platform allows traders to enter specific markets and allows the exit points for these trades. This strategy minimizes the losses of the trader, by focusing on trades that have the highest likelihood of turning a profit. While this may seem like an ineffective way of trading, it is a very effective way for the novice or experienced traders who do not wish to deal with the uncertainty of live market trading.

Coinbase has developed several other apps as well. The most well-known is the android app, which allows its users to buy and sell their favorite crypto coins, as well as trade in the market themselves. Their iPhone app also allows users to buy and sell their favorite currencies from anywhere they are. The web-based desktop app gives users the ability to view their entire portfolio through the Chrome browser, as well as viewing their market data from anywhere in the world.

Another great feature of the coinbase application is its newsfeed. What you can do is install the Coinbase desktop wallet, which will grant you access to all the coins listed on the exchanges. Once this is done, you will be able to monitor the value of your portfolio through the Coinbase home page. You can also subscribe to the Coinbase news feed, which will give you the latest updates about the value of your chosen currency pair. It is important to keep yourself informed about the current market, as this can allow you to make better decisions for your investment portfolio.

All in all, the best part about using the Coinbase platform to trade in all cryptocurrencies like Bitcoin and Altcoins is that you can do so without having to pay a single penny to trade. This is because a cryptocurrency can be exchanged directly for another cryptocurrency without the need to convert to US dollars or any other fiat currency. However, even if you are trading from altcoin to altcoin, most governments consider this a 'taxable' event. So it's best to keep track of all your trades and consult an accountant who specializes in cryptocurrencies to assist you further during tax time.

Overall, Coinbase is a good choice for the everyday investor who wants to accumulate altcoins for the long term. With this exchange, you can also move your cryptocoins offline to a secure hardware wallet for long-term savings.

Chapter 37 – Cryptocurrency Wallets - What Are The Benefits and Drawbacks?

The first thing to know about Cryptocurrency Storage is that this is something that can be done using two different methods. The two types of Cryptocurrency Storage are offline and online. For people who like the offline storage method, there are a couple of choices here. One option is that you can put all your funds into a password-protected offline wallet, and then access it from a computer that has internet access (just like your home computer). Another option is to buy hardware wallets that act just like digital wallets except they don't have any sensitive information on them like passwords.

Now that we know what Cryptocurrency Storage is, we can move on to how to store bitcoins and altcoins in these wallets. One thing that you might want to keep in mind is that this is sensitive information that needs to be kept extremely safe. That means that you should do the job of securing these things, not just lightly downloading some software and storing it away in a drawer. There are some things that you should do to the best cold storage wallets.

The first thing that you want to do is run an antivirus program on your computer to make sure that it is clean. Now, the best way to go about this is to get a program that will work to both protect your computer from malicious software and prevent it from getting anything on it that could harm it. You need to search for some of the more reputable online companies that sell such programs. You may be able to find one within your price range by looking on the internet. If you decide to try out the free ones, make sure that they are properly encrypted before giving them away.

The next thing that you should do is set up a backup for your entire computer. This is probably the most important of the Cryptocurrency Storage Methods. If you are using one of the different storage methods for storing bitcoins and altcoins, then you have to ensure that they are not going to get lost or corrupted somehow. This can be quite difficult if you are not accustomed to how the software works. If you store them using a hot wallet, then there is very little chance of them being lost or corrupted, but if you use a cold storage method, then even this is somewhat of a remote possibility.

Some of the better-known options for this are desktop wallets as well as online services that allow you to keep all your private details on the computer as well as at your fingertips on a remote server. Many advantages come with using these as opposed to other Cryptocurrency Storage Methods. One of the main advantages is that they are extremely easy to use and you do not need to go through a series of procedures to set them up. You can open the wallet, transfer funds, and then be done with it.

This also means that you will not have to deal with any problems like forgetting about a receipt so you end up spending money on something you did not intend on buying in the first place. Many people that have cold storage options tend to forget about them because they do not have the benefit of being connected to the internet. With the use of offline hardware wallets, this is no longer a problem. They are connected to the internet only when you want.

The most common hardware storage wallets recommended for safe and secure long-term storage are Trezor and Ledger Nano. However, be sure to spend some time reading the information on their websites carefully to ensure you are using these important crypto-storage products correctly.

Chapter 38 - A New Transparency in the Lives of Cryptocurrency Consumers

Use TREZOR as a hardware wallet for bitcoins and other cryptocoins Digital currencies such as bitcoins are experiencing a surge in popularity over the years. They offer a high degree of privacy and as a result, they are becoming a serious option to store wealth. However, with this TREZOR hardware wallet, you'll go for the first and probably most popular version in this field. Learn the safest and most used method to store and above all, withdraw Bitcoins.

Trezor is one of the leading manufacturers of this type of hardware wallet for all major forms of digital currencies. Their TREZOR software is among the most sophisticated and advanced available.

If you own altcoins you may consider a paper wallet rather than a Trezor hardware wallet. This way you don't even need a laptop or PC to carry your treasured possessions around. But then you can't be too careful these days. You never know if someone out there is out to steal your coins! A Trezor device will ensure that nobody else can access your private information because the device itself is encrypted and safe from prying eyes.

There are a few advantages as to why you should use Trezor instead of other similar devices such as Ledger cards and paper wallets. A major advantage of using a Trezor paper wallet over the alternative is that you can view your account anytime you like. With Ledger cards and smartphones you must physically access your private information to check it, whereas with a Trezor you can view your account whenever you like.

A Trezor One hardware wallet also supports a large number of cryptocurrencies and the list continues to grow as new coins come onto the market. It's impressive really because, with the other wallets and cards on the market, only a handful of currencies can be supported. Trezor almost supports every single one.

There is no doubt that Trezor has some of the most cutting-edge technology available for backing tokens and coins. The Trezor hardware wallet is available for Trezor Mobile Platform, Trezor Web Wallet, Trezor Enterprise Wallet, and the Trezor Go wallet. No matter what your needs, you're sure to find something that works well with your mobile device. You can store your tokens and coins on your phone, your tablet, your laptop, or even your desktop computer! Trezor goes beyond traditional passwords and account security by integrating with the android native code, so your information is always protected. The password manager, password change, and identity manager included in the Trezor Ecosystem make managing your tokens and coins a breeze.

Chapter 39 - Advantages Of Nano Ledger Software Wallets

A new revolution in the field of currency is the Nano Ledger. The future is here, it is time to shift to new technologies that will make the future. The Nano Ledger is the first new kind of digital asset that is entirely secured by using the ledger technology called Nano Ledger Technology.

This revolutionary innovation is all set to revolutionize the way transactions are processed in the financial industry. It is the next generation of ledger design, combining the benefits of a traditional Ledger with the advantages of a smartphone. This technological innovation aims at bringing real-time recording and accounting capabilities to organizations that are committed to making their business more transparent and accountable. Based on the latest secure chip technology for top-level security.

It connects to a smartphone (or any other device using a USB connection for optimal security) and displays an interactive OLED display on the front side for double-checking and confirming each transaction with just a single touch on its multi-color touch-sensitive side buttons. Multi-currencies, multi-applications, verified asset delivery, etc. Transactions are recorded in real-time and account owners can view the account summary and transaction history through their smartphones from anywhere in the world. Transactions are also secured by the use of fingerprint scanning for account owners. Account management is made simpler for all account holders with the help of this latest innovation.

Transactions are recorded in the form of an encrypted image or the transaction block which can be deciphered from the device with the help of the Nano Ledger Software. This secure device is equipped with all the latest tools for instant encryption/decryption. All information is encrypted and protected with advanced Firmware encryption. The ledger can be accessed from any location with an internet connection. This enables all business activities to be carried out wherever the user is across the globe.

The main features of this device include ease of use, multi-currencies support, verified asset delivery, etc. Transactions can be carried out on all the major and most active currency pairs. This is because the Nano Ledger Apps can be installed in the Chrome browser or downloaded onto any iOS or Android device for secure and private use. There are no limits as to how many accounts can be opened on the Nano Ledger and thus all transactions take place instantly.

The Ledger Nano Apps can also be installed onto any of the five hardware devices like; USB flash drives, smart cards, secure electronic keys, and Tizen os or smartphones. Hence these Ledger Nano Apps can be easily transported from one device to another. Hence the Nano Ledger is ideally suited to any business activity that requires the secure storage of confidential or personally secures financial information. These devices do not require physical damage or any kind of hardware or software errors.

The installation process of the Nano Ledger is very easy. This can be done using the device driver software downloaded from the web. Once installed you need to configure your Nano Ledger to connect to a computer or a smartphone via USB or Bluetooth. You can also opt for ethernet if your network does not support wireless.

The Nano Ledger can hold up to two thousand coins and thus provides the users with a convenient and extremely valuable service. Since these devices can be used anywhere, even while traveling, they become handy for corporate accounts as well as other high-risk individual financial transactions. Businesses that process large volumes of cash can get a huge benefit from using this type of software wallet. Since the Nano Ledger App can be programmed to store oracle, privy to various other functions, it becomes ideal for the financial industry. Thus the software wallets can fulfill multiple roles in the financial market.

PART 5 – CONCLUSION: WHO WINS THE BATTLE OF ATLCOINS VS THE BITCOIN KING?

In this final part of this book, let's do a quick review, look into what are some of the best choices for investing in cryptos and we'll answer that pressing question of who wins the battle of the cryptocurrencies.

Chapter 40 – More About Altcoins – The Alternative Cryptocurrencies

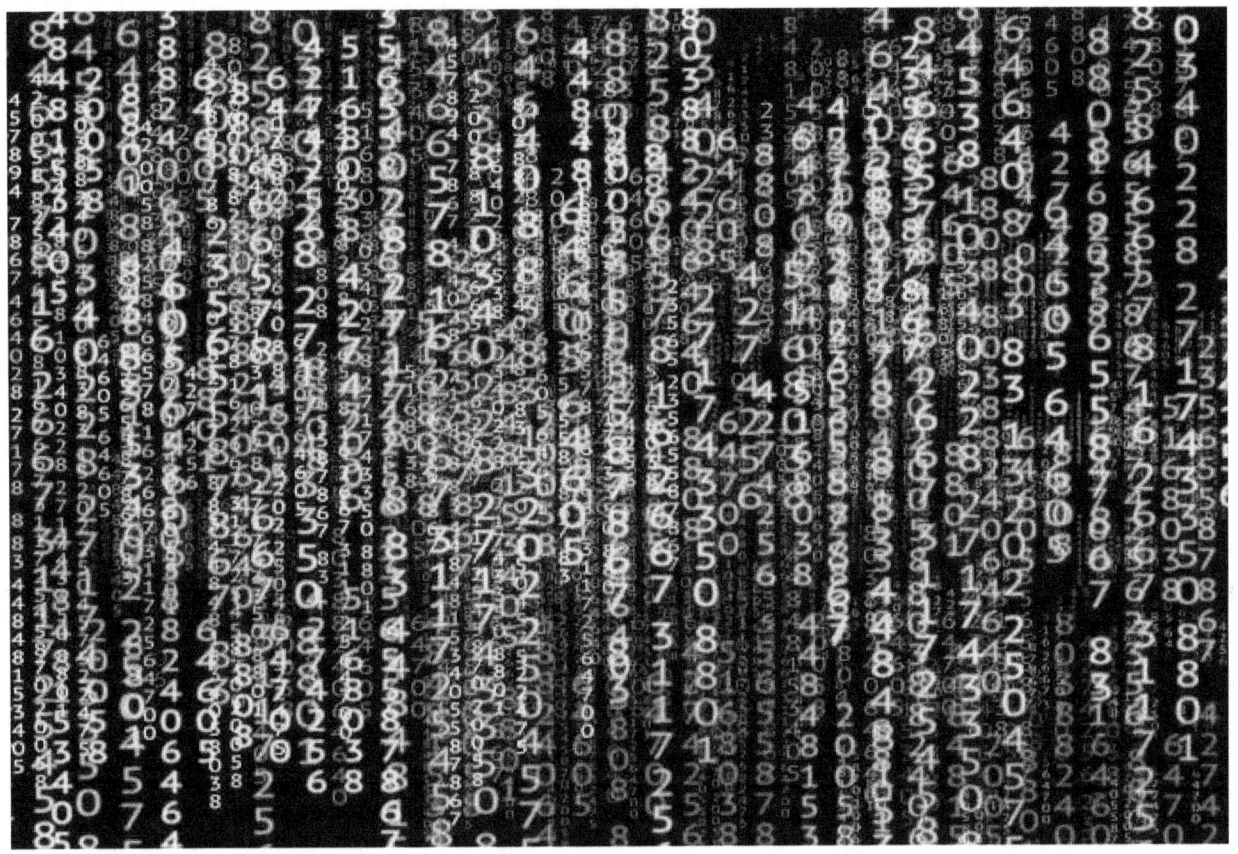

Altcoin can refer to any type of alternative Cryptocurrency other than Bitcoin. Simply put, they are virtual alternatives to Bitcoin. Both use similar infrastructure to allow you to create safe, secure peer-to-peer trades. But how does altcoin differ from traditional currencies?

One major difference is in the underlying infrastructure. Both rely on a ledger system called the blockchain to track all transactions. However, while most traditional cryptosystems allow you to create smart contracts, or BCPs, which are applications that run on top of the existing protocol, altcoins offer a way for crypto fans to create self-contained smart contracts or UTX. These smart contracts run completely separate from the underlying protocol and are usually implemented as security tokens.

This separation provides significant advantages for traders. An altcoin will always be priced a little lower than the price of bitcoins, as the speculators will always want to buy in at a lower cost. Therefore, it is possible to earn some revenue by providing traders with these types of investments. The ability to implement smart contracts also provides a valuable opportunity to implement smart contracts within the wider altcoin framework.

But there are also risks associated with investing in altcoins. This is because there is very little risk tolerance when it comes to the initial investment. Few experienced traders make a consistent profit from this form of investing. Fortunately, this doesn't mean that there are no opportunities. On the contrary, the number of emerging ICO As is increasing, therefore there is an increasing likelihood that investors will find a good and reliable platform to invest in.

If we look at some of the bigger names in the market today, we can see that the biggest winners come from the altcoins discussed in this book (with the notable exception of the stablecoins with fixed prices relative to fiat currency). While it may not seem like much of a surprise, these relatively new altcoins in the top 15 crypto market cap are enjoying strong growth. If nothing else, it helps that the developers behind these currencies are extremely creative and progressive. This is something that investors do not always find in the altcoin and ICO space, and this is very important to consider as you look for the best opportunities in the future. As always, the best bet for traders is to consult with experts and professionals in the field to determine which direction is right for you and stay up to date with the latest crypto news online. With enough practice in trading small amounts of cryptocurrencies, in time, you may become an expert yourself. For the average person not interested in constant trading, cryptocurrency investing maybe your best option. Whether you invest in top altcoins, bitcoin, or another newer cryptocurrency, be sure that you are doing so with the proper research and facts to back up your investment decisions.

Chapter 41 - A Brief Review of Cryptocurrencies

Cryptocurrencies are digital currencies that have grown in popularity in recent years. There is a whole world of Altcoins out there with their very own unique uses, however, bitcoins and ether are perhaps the most well-known. Investing in Cryptocurrencies has always been somewhat synonymous with investing in bitcoins, particularly for people new to this digital asset space. However, ether comes in at a very close second in this regard. It's not just because ether is cheap and fast to trade; it is also because ether has the distinct characteristics that set it apart from other currencies.

One of the biggest differences between an ordinary currency and a good volatile value coin like ether is that it doesn't have a conventional management system. This is one of the reasons why many investors are flocking towards these coins as they have the appeal of being free from any kind of government control or management. Investors can trade these currencies based on their perceived volatility. And when you consider the fact that most investors don't understand the underlying economics of the market, it is no big secret that volatility is the best way to trade.

When looking at the best currencies to invest in, one must keep the fundamentals in mind. That means that investors must be cognizant of their inherent values so that they can make investment decisions. Here are some of the best ways that investors can use to track the value of their chosen coins:

Actual Cost: The cost of any given transaction is important to investors who want to minimize their risk. This is especially true when it comes to investing in Cryptocurrencies due to the high liquidity factor. When a buyer wants to buy one unit of a particular currency, he or she will usually be buying a lot of it. Therefore, the transaction fee that they pay should be calculated in terms of the market cap or amount of the investment.

Decentralized Funds: Investing in decentralized funds is one of the best methods of securing finances for the long term. Several currencies can be chosen, but the most popular ones include those discussed in this book. Some lesser-known currencies are beginning to see a surge in popularity. However, the newer initial coin offerings and new cryptocoins on the market are usually riskier and more speculative plays, so we won't discuss these in detail here, especially since there are 1000s of altcoins available. These cryptocurrencies are not stored by the central authorities but rather are stored by decentralized exchanges that have reduced fees and commission while increasing liquidity. So if you are looking to secure finances for the future, investing in decentralized finance is a great way to go.

Initial Coin Offerings (ICO): If you want to get into the crypto sphere but aren't sure how to go about it, then look no further than the world of initial coin offerings. These are very popular online today, and they can be very profitable when handled properly. In simple terms, this process allows investors to purchase a certain number of tokens at a certain price before they are made accessible to the general public. At first glance, ICO may seem very lucrative, but several downsides need to be looked into before any investor should dive into it.

Smart Contract Platforms: Many Cryptocurrencies follow smart contract protocols. The protocol determines how the supply and demand of Cryptocurrencies will function within the network. Investors who wish to trade in Cryptocurrectains should be very familiar with smart contract protocols because this is where the majority of their profits will come from. ICO's that do not follow smart contract protocols are prone to become vulnerable to hackers. SinceICO is the first of its kind, it is also prone to having inexperienced hackers attack the system.

Many diverse elements make up the landscape. As with any business venture, it is important to understand the risks and rewards associated with investing. By doing so, it is possible to choose the right Cryptocurrency to fit an individual or business needs. For more information about the different aspects of decentralized applications (DApps), it is suggested to consult with a financial advisor who specializes in this.

Chapter 42 - Using Dollar Cost Averaging Strategies For Your Crypto Portfolio

Dollar-cost averaging is an investment technique that can give you extra cash flow, and it can be used in cryptocurrency investing the same way that it can be used for investing in stocks. Sounds like a no-brainer right? Why would anyone want to invest all of that money all at one time? There are tons of reasons someone could use to do this, but the benefits of doing it are very powerful. I am going to discuss some benefits below.

One of the biggest benefits of dollar-cost averaging is that it increases your ability to gain favorable long-term asset allocation. Let's say you got your bonus last week and you now have $4k you want to invest for the future. If you were able to invest that amount in the cryptocurrencies you care about throughout the year then you would have a much better return than if you invested half of your bonus money into these cryptocurrencies. The better returns come from choosing your investment right but you also want to increase your ability to gain the asset allocation you want.

This benefit also applies to dollar-cost averaging with stocks (still a good choice, if you do your research), or mutual funds (not recommended, but there are plenty of other books on this). Most of the time when people try to choose their investment they make the common mistake of trying to pick the "winners" or the best-performing stocks. The reality is that most of the time the best-performing stocks are not even in the top 10% of the overall stock market, (and the same can be said of temporary runners in the crypto market). It is very difficult to get a solid percentage share of a company's stock because there are so many other investors trying to dump shares of the company. By doing your research and choosing the best-performing stocks you can do your part by diversifying your portfolio.

Another of the benefits of dollar cost averaging in both cryptocurrencies and stocks is that you can often reduce your total cost of ownership at any given time. This is great especially if you are constantly having trouble getting high dollar-cost averaging percentage shares. Dollar-cost averaging gives you the ability to spread out the overall costs of your investments in your investment account. You just need to make sure you are using a low-dollar cost averaging strategy versus an aggressive strategy.

Probably one of the biggest benefits of dollar-cost averaging when it comes to crypto investing is that it will help protect you during a market crash. What happens is that during a major market crash people tend to panic. This causes them to sell off their bitcoins and altcoins at lightning-fast prices. If you have a diversified crypto portfolio, it will help you protect your capital as well. Since the market crash is typically bad for everybody this is one of the greatest benefits of dollar-cost averaging for your investing strategy.

One more of the benefits of dollar-cost averaging with cryptocurrency is that it will help you make sure your risk versus reward profile stays intact. In a major market crash, investors tend to sell off their cryptocurrencies and stocks just before things turn in the negative direction. This causes a lot of short-term losses for individual investors. However, if you stick with your cryptocurrencies during this period you can usually manage quite well. Your dollar-cost averaging strategy will offset any losses that you incur and help protect you from any large gains that might occur at the start of the market crash. The key is to make sure you are diversified throughout the period of time that you are investing.

Of course, another benefit of dollar-cost averaging when it comes to investments is that it allows you to avoid selling off all of your crypto shares every time the market changes. Every time you buy bitcoins or altcoins you are essentially incurring a purchase expense on your part. If you were to only buy cryptos when they were at a value that is lower than what you paid for them you would be incurring quite a bit of cash buying cryptos at market value. With this strategy, you avoid the cash outlay associated with buying all of your cryptocurrencies at regular intervals.

The main reason that many investors choose to use a dollar-cost averaging strategy is because of the way the market fluctuates. It doesn't follow that an altcoin that goes up one day will always go up or down the next. Most investors who are new to investing in cryptocurrencies or stocks will often lose money from time to time. This is not because their portfolio is bad or because they don't know how to manage the portfolio. Rather, most investors make mistakes because they are unfamiliar with the ups and downs of the market. For this reason, many investors will just let their portfolio ride out the ups and downs of the market, and this is where dollar-cost averaging can really help you out.

Chapter 43 - Using More Dollar Cost Averaging Strategies

Dollar-cost averaging is an effective and simple investing technique. Instead of finding the right time to purchase and sell a particular asset, dollar-cost averaging instead simplifies investing by concentrating on regularly investing a set amount of cash into your overall portfolio over a long period of time. In a traditional investing approach, you would set aside some money, invest it, and wait to see what the value of your investments would be at a certain point in time. The problem with this is that numerous factors could affect the value of your investments. Also, there are various rules and regulations in place to ensure that the money you are putting into the market isn't at risk of losing value.

With a dollar-cost averaging investment strategy, you can follow the rules of investing and reap the benefits from your investments while minimizing your potential losses. This type of investing technique has been around for decades but only recently has it gained in popularity among more seasoned traders. The reason is mainly due to the rise in the value of the popularly known Bitcoins and Altcoins These types of assets tend to be highly volatile because they are highly influenced by factors such as supply and demand. If you can minimize the influence of these factors then you will be able to maximize your profits in a much shorter period of time.

Another major benefit associated with this style of investing is that it is relatively low risk. In a traditional investing approach, you would typically have to either diversify your assets and hope that your stock or bond would appreciate or you would have to sit on your investment and hope that it would do well enough to give you a decent profit. However, with this type of strategy, you can follow the rules and reap the rewards from your investments in a reasonable time frame. For this reason, the dollar-cost averaging strategy may be particularly appealing to cryptocurrency investors. This type of investing strategy also tends to be rather easy to learn which makes it appealing to a lot of people who are just starting with their investment portfolios.

With dollar-cost averaging strategies, many people can realize their maximum profit over time. It is also a great way for new investors to learn about the dynamics involved in these types of investments. Many newbie traders focus on only one or two types of assets while they are still learning about the business. Unfortunately, this often results in bad investment decisions due to not being able to fully understand the implications of their investment choices. You can make the most money if you combine several different types of investments over time. Even the most experienced investors often make mistakes due to unexpected turns in the market. With dollar-cost averaging and a diverse portfolio of bitcoin and top altcoins, it is more likely that the drawdowns will be averaged out in the end.

One great example of a combination of several popular assets is the use of dollar-cost averaging with the use of recurring buys. Using recurring buys will allow you to exploit the fluctuating value of cryptocurrencies. This information is very valuable for many investors who are looking to capitalize on global economics and the political news that frequently affects these commodities. When combined with dollar-cost averaging strategies, you will most likely be able to see your investments grow over time due to the consistent increase in the value of the cryptocurrencies.

The best way to start using the combination of strategies is to first purchase a set amount worth of investments each month. You will then spread them out amongst several different accounts that have similar characteristics. By doing this, you will find that you will be able to get the best returns on your investment dollar-cost averaging. You can also diversify between different types of digital assets, and in addition to cryptocurrencies, you may want to also include other assets such as stocks, bonds, and commodities full a fully diversified portfolio. In general, due to the unpredictability of future markets, it is not recommended to invest more than 5 to 10% of your income and/or net worth in cryptocurrencies. Fortunately, if cryptocurrencies keep rising at their current rates, even a small investment today or throughout this year could become very valuable indeed in the years ahead.

To maximize the potentials of the dollar-cost averaging strategies, you should also add ethereal into the mix. The combination of factors will help you realize maximum profits even if you are holding an investment in several different currencies. Since e Ethereum is currently the second most profitable currency that is being traded on the market, you will want to make sure that you are diversifying your investments across all of the currencies that are related to ethereal. This will help to ensure that you do not lose any money from one currency and yet profit from another when the market fluctuates between the currencies.

As an investor, you must keep in mind that when you are selecting which currencies to invest in, you must take into account both the long-term and short-term aspects. Long-term considerations involve the health of the cryptocurrency economy, its overall strength, the stability of the government, and the inflation rate. Oddly enough, deflationary cryptocurrencies such as Bitcoins and most of the Altcoins discussed in this book tend to rise when the dollar experiences inflation. This is because these top cryptocurrencies (with exception of stablecoins) have a limited supply, whereas dollar printing by the government is potentially unlimited. Short-term aspects entail the volatility of the market, investor confidence, and trader's expectations. Always consider the impact of these factors when selecting the cryptocurrencies to invest in and when best to use dollar-cost averaging strategies to diversify the investments and minimize risk.

Chapter 44 - Dollar Cost Averaging: A Great Option For Long Term Investing

As a brief review, dollar cost averaging is an investment strategy that many people are turning to as a means of achieving financial stability. What is dollar-cost averaging and how does it work? The simple explanation is this: instead of investing money one by one, investors invest their money into a basket of cryptocurrencies. Once each cryptocurrency reaches a certain dollar amount, this basket is divided up and invested somewhere else until the desired goal is reached.

The primary benefit of dollar-cost averaging (DCA) is that most investors don't have to hold any physical assets in order to partake in the plan. Instead, the entire plan can simply be implemented as a safety stop, assuming that the desired price targets are reached. There is also the additional benefit that investors in the future will be able to buy into currencies when they are far less valuable than they are today. This is because bitcoin and top altcoin assets will likely be worth considerably more in a few years.

While the idea of dollar-cost averaging can be applied to several different investment strategies, one of the best ones that the e-commerce industry can utilize is their ethereal Asset Management. Just like DSA, investing in ether is seen as a long-term venture. While there is still a learning curve associated with this strategy, it is a strategy that has the potential to grow significantly over time. In this chapter, we will take a closer look at the reasons why eCommerce and investors alike should consider the use of dollar-cost averaging for their Crypto Asset Management.

While it may seem like investing in the dollar-cost averaging daily is a good idea, it can turn out to be a bad move if an investor invests too much money into the market. Since the market contains large swings, it is not uncommon for the value of one security to change drastically from the previous day. If an investor tends to chase down every little movement, he or she may miss out on some of the better price movements. When looking at how the various factors are affecting the market, there is no reason why an investor should ever invest in a single cryptocurrency daily. Instead, the best option is to diversify the way that investor funds for his or her portfolio and the best way to do this is to use a low-volatility investing strategy. For this reason, implementing a dollar-cost averaging strategy should include regular investments on a weekly or monthly time frame.

One way to do this involves using a combination of moderate-risk but high potential crypto investments. For advanced traders, this can include both long and short positions, and when an investor pairs the two he or she will be taking on a higher risk than if they invested solely in the dollar-cost averaging scheme. For the Altcoin beginner, it is recommended just to stick with regular buy (long) orders, and avoid overcomplicating your trading with short selling orders which some advanced traders may use.

The goal of diversifying the portfolio is to support investors' ability to ride out any waves caused by changes in global conditions, which can also help to protect assets from becoming too volatile and imperiled.

Chapter 45 - Making Long Term Crypto Investments

In the future, there will be more people who are interested in learning how to collect crypto coins. People like your friends and family will want to know what they can do to accumulate cryptocurrencies, and now you'll be able to refer them to this book.

Generally speaking, if you are holding a well-diversified cryptocurrency investment position over a longer time, then you may begin to introduce a few more slightly speculative investments into your overall portfolio mix. That's because you could (theoretically) tolerate a small bit of fluctuation in market value with the hope that over time the good times will balance out for your profit. But what if the market value does not perform according to your expectations? In that case, you would either need to cut your losses or re-evaluate your entire strategy. Fortunately, by diversifying in a variety of top Altcoins plus the Bitcoin King, and by implementing an effective dollar-cost averaging strategy, you are more than likely to come out ahead over the long term.

Now one of the difficulties with speculative long-term investments like new ICO altcoins is how to identify when they might outperform the market in terms of performance. It is important to remember that all of these are dynamic, always changing, and subject to large changes in the current environment. A portfolio that is designed to take advantage of current market fluctuations will probably not fare well in years to come. This is why you must have some way of gauging how these investments are performing. Fortunately, this is not as difficult as it seems with a good cryptocurrency broker such as Binance.com, Binance.us or Coinbase.com. Just be sure to check your account statements regularly to ensure that cryptocurrencies are performing as expected.

Of course, some categories of long-term investments are much riskier than others. For example, speculative ICO altcoins are considered to be a high risk, but potentially high return investment, so this is something that you want to avoid as a beginner. However, as you become more experienced and understand more about the different kinds of novel cryptocoin investments that you are interested in, these speculative investments can play a very important role. If you do choose to invest in speculative ICO altcoins, then just be sure to limit their weighting in your crypto portfolio, so that ideally they do not exceed more than 10% of all your crypto. It is recommended that the remainder of your portfolio consist of top-performing, well-established altcoins as well as Bitcoin.

It's also very important that you think about your retirement planning and the time horizon that you have in mind for retirement. If you are looking to make long-term investments in the crypto market, you will certainly want to use the right crypto exchange broker to do so. However, not all crypto brokers can provide you with access to all of the cryptocurrencies that are available in the markets you want to invest in. In addition, some exchanges only offer a small selection of the many different types of cryptocurrencies that are available and might not provide all of the information that you need to make an informed decision. A good investment strategy will always involve having a long-term investment plan in place as well as being knowledgeable about your own individual retirement goals, in addition to using a reputable crypto exchange such as those discussed earlier.

Once you have taken the time to learn about the various types of long-term crypto investments that you should and shouldn't invest in, and you have developed a solid investment strategy, you should have a better idea of what types of long-term investments that you should be making. Knowing these types of investments will go a long way in ensuring that you are always staying invested in the crypto markets.

Remember to also check www.coinmarketcap.com on a regular basis, to see which altcoins are challenging for the #1 spot currently held by the Bitcoin King. As with any investment, knowledge is key, and keeping yourself informed and up-to-date about all of your crypto investment choices will ensure that you are making the right decisions about where to put your money.

Chapter 46 - Benefits of Investing in Cryptocurrencies

There are now over 5,000 Altcoins cryptocurrencies out there. While in general, you can use Cryptocurrency to purchase items, most wise folks generally only treat it as an investment. Hopefully, this book has helped guide you through the process to help ensure you have a positive experience. In this final chapter, we will discuss some important considerations when considering Cryptocurrencies for long-term investments.

Many experts agree that investing 5 to 10% of your portfolio in cryptocurrencies is a wise investment for the long term.

Keep in mind that some altcoin cryptocurrencies are unpredictable, and some have the potential to become worthless.

It is unlikely that the top 15 discussed in this book will become worthless, but it's an important precaution to keep in mind that no one knows what the future holds exactly. So don't risk investing more than you can afford to lose.

If you invest in altcoin cryptocurrencies carelessly, you could lose your shirt, so be careful. However, if you invest wisely, (for example by rereading this book again carefully), top altcoins and bitcoins can have the potential to make you a fortune in the years ahead.

There are many advantages to investing in Cryptocurrencies such as Bitcoin, Ethereum, Cardano, Binance Coin, Ripple, Dogecoin, Polkadot, Solana, Uniswap, Bitcoin Cash, Litecoin, Chainlink, among other top altcoins. Many of these cryptocurrencies function very much like traditional money. They are backed by digital assets and mathematical algorithms and therefore are secure just as gold and silver coins are. One big difference between Cryptocurrencies and traditional investments is the way they are traded. Unlike stocks and bonds, which usually trade on stock exchanges, cryptocurrencies can only be bought or sold on specialized crypto exchanges that are either centralized (like Binance or Coinbase) or decentralized (like Uniswap).

This means that instead of trading shares, you are trading digital coins. This also allows you to leverage your investment because you can control a great deal of value at any given time. Investing in Cryptocurrencies might not be suitable for those who are new to the markets or those who are uncomfortable with the technology and computer science behind these currencies. For example, if you are interested in putting money into stocks, you would need to understand the mechanics of the stock market to even start considering investing in currencies. The same can be said of investing in cryptocurrencies.

On the other hand, for beginners, intermediates, or advanced investors who have read this book, there are many benefits associated with investing in cryptocurrencies. In many cases, with the blockchain technology that is involved in crypto investments, it is much faster and easier to get up to speed on Cryptocurrencies than it would be to understand, use and manage some traditional investments. Many Cryptocurrencies are also extremely liquid which makes it easy even for novices to get in (or out) of the market almost whenever they want.

There are many benefits of investing in Cryptocurrencies including their relatively low cost and diversification of investment risk. Also, due to the distributed nature of these cryptocurrencies, there is very little hacking possible which can be a major concern for companies and governments. In addition, with the rising number of users, it is possible for anyone to start investing in the future of Cryptocurrencies which also provides investors with a wide range of opportunities. In general, by using the distributed ledger technology behind blockchains, it is possible to enjoy the benefits of ICO along with the cost efficiency and diversity of investing into most of the top fifteen most traded Cryptocurrencies.

Bitcoin will always hold the title of the first and original cryptocurrency. However, as we've seen throughout this book it does have some challengers for the number one spot. Bitcoin currently has the advantage of name recognition and market prominence, but there are potential competitors that can displace it in the future. No one knows for certain whether Bitcoin will be displaced, or which Altcoin will take its place. Since the future is always printing at the hard right edge of your cryptocurrency trading charts, it remains unknown until the future arrives. In the meantime, it may be a wise decision to diversify your portfolio with a variety of Altcoins discussed in this book, and just let the future marketplace decide who emerges the victor. In the end, if most of the cryptocurrencies in the top 15 market capitalization continue to increase in value against the fiat currencies of the globe, then dollar-cost averaging of a diverse portfolio of top Altcoins in addition to the Bitcoin King could very well be the best investment strategy.

As we've seen throughout this book, bitcoin and altcoins have a variety of uses and features. Ultimately, over time the marketplace will determine each of their true values. And the altcoin that proves to be the most valuable to the marketplace could potentially someday displace the Bitcoin King. Until then, the future of cryptocurrency continues to look promising, although the future remains unwritten.

www.ingramcontent.com/pod-product-compliance
Lightning Source LLC
LaVergne TN
LVHW081539060526
838200LV00048B/2139